Guillaume's storytelling reign continues:

Guillaume is the Dave Barry of the SCA. I eagerly look forward to (reading) his articles. His irreverent, off-the-wall humor about the game we all love usually has me doubled up laughing. Yet there is often a gentle bit of education in his articles, and frequently a reminder of the ideals of courtesy and honor we hold dear. Guillaume's writing guides us as it entertains us. It doesn't get any better than that.

> Baronessa Francesca di Pavia, OP, OL, President SCA Inc., *Outlands*

Guillaume's keen observations may be cloaked in humor, but you get much more out of his work than mere laughs. He offers himself as guide to a world filled with wonder—the one we all live in—if you simply look at it through his eyes. Sometimes irreverent, often insightful, *always* entertaining.

> Baron Bran Trefonnen, OL, OP, *Ansteorra*

Any recipe for a well-balanced retreat into the Current Middle Ages has to include a respectable amount of self-reflection, a healthy dose of Truth, Trust and Honor, and a slew of Special Moments that touch the Heart. But none of it would make any sense if we forgot to see the humor in what we do and how we do it. Guillaume's view is the spicy Chivalric garnish that makes the whole recipe work for me. For if we cannot belly laugh at ourselves, how can we even begin to take ourselves seriously?

> Duchess Katerina O'Callaghan, OP, *Atenveldt*

I have met very few people who can tell a story like Guillaume. Even fewer can relate the Current Middle Ages to our everyday experiences as well as he can. Even fewer than that can make me laugh and think really hard at the same time. Those in the SCA enjoy how he can get to the heart of the organization and help us understand why we do this, and how fun it is to be very silly at a sometimes very serious game. Those who have no idea what the Current Middle Ages is about are in for a treat. You don't have to be in the SCA or even be a history buff to enjoy and learn from his stories.

Mistress Heirusalem Crystoma, OP, Publisher of *The Pennsic Independent*, Kingdom Chronicler *Midrealm*

When reading Guillaume's hysterically funny writings, one could easily buy into the image he presents of himself: That he's only two rising snaps away from lobotomizing himself, but—look again. The ideas shared in Guillaume's tales don't come from the village idiot. Far from it. These SCA moments are poignant, well-written and give a glimpse at this Fine Game as played by one who clearly is aware of what is going on around him.

Baron Auguste Valizan, OP, former Kingdom Chronicler *Ealdormere*

Here Comes the Reign, Sir Guillaume!

Here Comes the Reign, Sir Guillaume!

◆

Another collection of warped, wicked and wild stories about medieval history and life in (and around) the SCA.

A second volume of the collected writings of Sir Guillaume de la Belgique

Scott A. Farrell

iUniverse, Inc.
New York Lincoln Shanghai

Here Comes the Reign, Sir Guillaume!
Another collection of warped, wicked and wild stories about medieval history and life in (and around) the SCA.

Copyright © 2005 by Scott A. Farrell

All rights reserved. No part of this book may be used or reproduced by any means, graphic, electronic, or mechanical, including photocopying, recording, taping or by any information storage retrieval system without the written permission of the publisher except in the case of brief quotations embodied in critical articles and reviews.

iUniverse books may be ordered through booksellers or by contacting:

iUniverse
2021 Pine Lake Road, Suite 100
Lincoln, NE 68512
www.iuniverse.com
1-800-Authors (1-800-288-4677)

Page art by Diane Lynn
First edition, March 2005

ISBN: 0-595-34686-3

Printed in the United States of America

For those who made the laughter, labor and love possible: Wulfric and Veronique, Hrodnavar and Ceridwen, and their crews of miracle-workers, far too numerous to mention, but fully appreciated and respected, always.

◆ ◆ ◆

And to my wonderful duchess, wife and friend, the most noble person to ever wear a Crown, Felinah.

Contents

Introduction: When We Left Our Hero... 1

The Ground Rules Or Introduction, Part 2 4

Hey, Ho, the Wind and the Reign or Postcards From The Throne, Part 1. 7

To Find the SCA, Just Turn Right at Spiderman 11

A Knight's Castle Is His Home. 16

Time And Space. 20

Purple Reign or Postcards From The Throne, Part 2. 23

Why Crown Finals Will Never Be On ESPN 28

A Little Touch of SCA in Your Pocket 31

Spitting Distance From Chivalry. 34

Chronicles of the Inquisitor, Part 1 38

Comments From The Red Belt Gallery. 40

Of Arms and the Knight I Sing. 44

The Reign At Pennsic Falls Mainly On The Plain or Postcards From The Throne, Part 3 49

Fangs For The Memories: Medieval Halloween Monsters. 54

The Romance of the Sword. 58

Chronicles of the Inquisitor, Part 2. 62

School of Hard Knatts. 65

The Dramatic Lessons of History............................ 69
Reigny Days and Mondays or Postcards From The Throne, Part 4 ... 73
Knightly Attributes 78
Chronicles of the Inquisitor, Part 3 81
Just Another Knight On the Wall 84
The Christmas Crazies: Forgotten Medieval Holiday Traditions 88
There Is A Hole In Your Heart 92
Some Knights to Remember 95
Guillaume & Felinah—Wasn't That A Reign or The Last Postcard
    From The Throne.................................... 99
Finale... 105
About the Author 107

Here Comes the Reign, Sir Guillaume!

By Sir Guillaume "I Like My Men Like I Like My Coffee—Warm, Straight and Slightly Transparent" de la Belgique

Visit the author's website at:
www.SirGuillaume.com

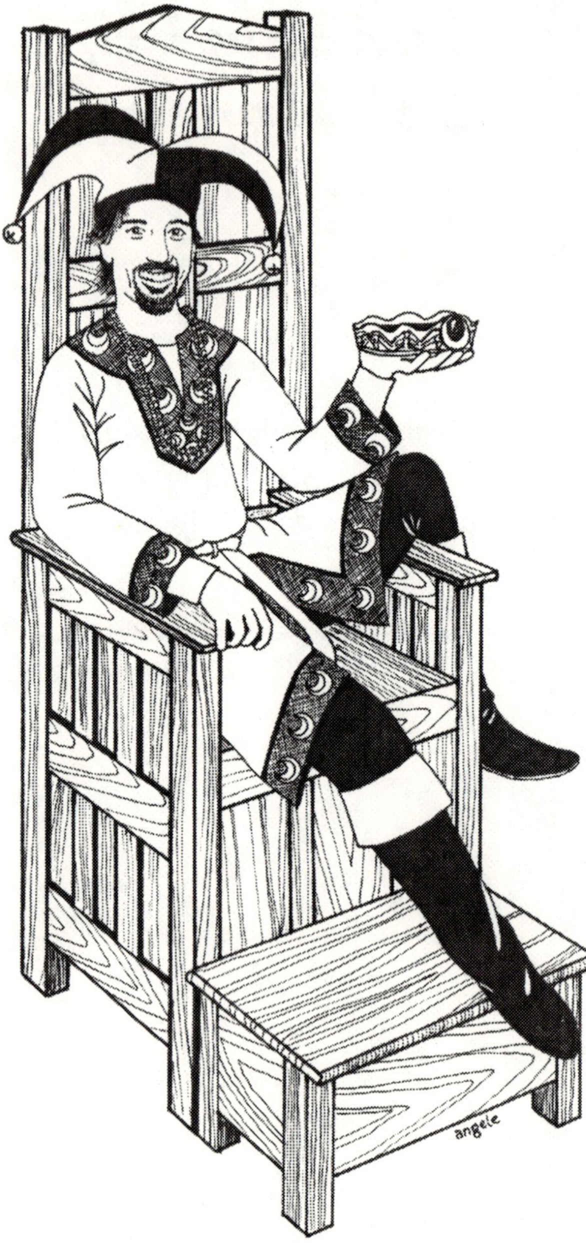
angele

Introduction:
When We Left Our Hero...

Those of you who've read my first book may recall that in the final chapter I described the decisive blow of the tournament in which, by some implausible disruption of the natural balance of the universe, I won the Crown of Caid. This book will pick up (roughly) where that one left off, but before getting started, I'd like to take a moment to A) welcome familiar friends and new readers alike, and B) emphasize one little thing that many people seem to have difficulty accepting when they read my stories:

Everything in this book is true.

Oh, I know what you're thinking. "Guillaume's taken quite a few head shots over the years. Clearly he's not thinking quite right any more. His stories, from warped interpretations of medieval history to outrageous yarns about life in the SCA, may be funny and entertaining...but they certainly aren't true, *are they?*"

Well, as a rather long-winded way of answering that question, let me explain what you're going to find on the pages that follow.

When I discovered the SCA, I was just 15 years old. A fellow named Gregory of York, who wore a shiny coronet and called himself a "duke," came to my high school to give a talk on medieval history for our social studies class. As part of this presentation, he let several students put on his helm (which was permanently infused with the delicate bouquet of epoxy glue and old sweat) and get hit in the head with a rattan sword.

Perhaps it was the glue fumes or the disorientation caused by a concussive head blow, but from that moment on, I somehow knew the SCA was a place I could call home. I also had this vague, nebulous notion that maybe, someday, I could get to be a "duke" myself. (I wasn't entirely sure what that meant, mind you, but I thought that leafy coronet was pretty cool!)

My first book, *We Are Not Amused, Sir Guillaume!*, was a compilation of the reflections, stories and essays I've written during my quarter-century in the Society about growing up and (hopefully) growing wise in the Current Middle Ages. It was my goal in that book to bring out the "universal elements" (if you'll allow me to use a grandiose, pretentious term) that make being in the SCA both amusing and delightful. I wanted to show how the SCA is, in many ways, "home" to us all.

In this, my second book, I'd like continue in that vein—with a little something "extra" thrown in besides.

In the chapters of this book, you'll find a wide variety of subjects covered. Some of the chapters will delve into the history, personalities and folklore of the *real* Middle Ages in order to show you that the axiom "truth is stranger than fiction" is more than just a cliché. Exploring the oddities, conflicts and biases of medieval society can be a fun way to learn a little more about history, but it's also a means of reminding ourselves that re-creating the broad palate of the medieval world, with its clashing colors (Vikings), expensive pigments (the Italians) and unwashable dyes (Scotsmen), is what makes the anachronistic cultural melting pot of the SCA so much fun.

Other chapters in this book will examine the Current Middle Ages for what it is: A *really* big fraternity of friends who gather to reaffirm their core values, such as the reward of service, the uplifting quality of respect, and the enjoyment of pummeling one another with sticks of rattan. From time to time, it's important to reflect fondly upon the things that drew us all to the Society in the first place, and in so doing remember that titles, awards and politics are nothing but byproducts of our involvement in the group.

Still other chapters will examine not what we bring *into* the Society, but what we *take away* from it. For all the staunch declarations that the SCA's weekend environment is "just a game," it's also important to realize that we don't set aside our ideals of compassion, reputation and responsibility when we hang up our garb on Sunday afternoon. The standards of chivalry and honor linger with us at our workplaces, in our classrooms and in our homes, helping us each in our own small way to make the world of the 21st century a better place. (In that way, the SCA "game" is a tribute to the words of Aristotle: "You can learn more about a person in an hour of play than in a year of conversation.")

To make this more than just a "rehash" of my first book, however, I would like to add something extra: The view from the top. In amongst the stories of fractured history, SCA antics and the ironies of being a "post-modern medievalist," I want to share with you a variety of reminiscences, scattered periodically throughout the book, about what it's like to wear a Crown and rule a kingdom—hopefully without ever losing sight of that boy sitting in the high school lecture hall thinking, "Wouldn't that be cool…"

In short, what I hope to do, in a series of essays spread throughout this book, is to take you on a journey, with laughter and tears, from "the ground to the Crown, and back again"—a trip that, in many ways, is a metaphor of the hopes, dreams and obligations we all pursue in every part of our lives. Although a few of the details of this journey may be "slightly exaggerated," I think you'll see that these stories are emotionally honest and authentic, because this book isn't about *one* king or *one* queen or even *one* kingdom. It's about all of us, from the person who has just attended his or her first event to reigning monarchs, respected peers and members of the Board of Directors. What I want to give you in this book is an exploration of that sense of majesty and purpose that keeps bringing us back to our tournaments, wars and revels, and that make this seemingly trivial hobby a lifelong passion.

Which may, or may not, lend credibility to my claim that what you'll read in this book is "real." For validation in that regard, I suspect I can do no better than to turn to the words of the famous 15th century publisher William Caxton, who, in the introduction to another moderately successful collection of stories about knights and kings, said:

> "For to pass the time this book shall be pleasant to read in; but for to give faith and believe that all is true, ye be at your liberty. Yet no exchanges shall ye have without thine original receipt."

Thanks for taking time to join me on this journey, for allowing me to do my best to entertain you with what little wit is left to me after 25 years of repeated head blows, and for doing your part to perpetuate this enchanted realm where The Dream rules us all, king and queen, knight, duke and commoner alike.

The Ground Rules
Or
Introduction, Part 2

Okay, I can hear my publisher howling: "Shut up already and get on with the book!"

Well, before we launch into the first chapter, there are a few things I want to spell out because it occurs to me the process of winning a Crown and being a monarch in the SCA may not be obvious to everyone, no matter how long you've been in the Society, or how many kings and queens you've seen. So, just to make sure we're all playing from the same sheet of music, here's a quick "Q&A" session that will address a few of the more common questions and misconceptions about royalty in the Current Middle Ages.

What does it mean to be "king" or "queen"?

With the assumption that we're looking for "meaning" in the technical, rather than the metaphysical sense, the official definition is that the king and queen are the ceremonial leaders of a regional division of the SCA Inc. Ironically, they have very little actual, legal, recognized-by-the-IRS authority, but they have a great deal of influence within the Society. It's a marvelous, but sometimes baffling study in social dynamics, and I'm sure that someday someone will write a brilliant thesis for their political science doctoral degree based on the conglomeration of modern, medieval and Tolkiensian fantasy governance we've created here. (And if there are any undergrads reading who want to use that idea, please contact me. My licensing fees are very reasonable.)

How do you get to be king?

SCA monarchs are chosen in a very un-medieval way: by a tournament. (There were never any rulers in the Middle Ages who attained their position by winning a sporting competition—unless you consider the Wars of the Roses to be a strange sort of soccer league with weapons.) Every six months, each regional division of the SCA (called a *kingdom*) puts on a *Crown Tournament*. The winner of that tournament immediately becomes the *crown prince*, or the *heir to the throne*. Then, after a period of time somewhere between a few weeks and several months, there is a *coronation* ceremony in which the old king and queen step down and the royal heirs are sworn in as the new monarchs.

Can a woman become king?

Despite criticisms that we've created a revisionist, gender-neutral version of the Middle Ages, in the SCA, where women can be knights and compete in tournaments, a woman *can* win a Crown, although she's referred to as a *sovereign queen*. In such a case, the king is called the *king consort*. (Throughout this book, however, I'm going to stick with the traditional "male dominated" terminology and risk the wrath of the many talented, dangerous female fighters whom I count among my friends. Getting pounded by Duchess Elina is much less painful than trying to proofread a bunch of funky "His and/or Her Majesty" royal pronouns.)

How do you get to be queen?

Prior to entering the lists of a Crown Tournament, every fighter must declare his or her *consort*—the person who will become queen (or king consort) should that warrior win the day's tournament. The choice of a consort may be based on romance, friendship or practicality—or, in the best of scenarios, all three. Whatever the case, during their reign, the "royal couple" will get to know one another very, very well—which is either going to make them particularly close and intimate, or make them never want to speak to each other again. (If you were really jaded, you might even say it's a lot like a marriage—but I'd never make such cynical statement.)

What happens when you're done being king and queen?

The king can't fight in a Crown Tournament, which means that a king and queen can't succeed themselves. Thus, there's an inferred "royal term limit" built into the Crown Tournament process, but former kings and queens aren't forgotten about. After his first reign a king is, upon stepping down, given the title of *count* (the queen gets the title of *countess*). After retiring from a second reign, the former king gets the title of *duke* (and the queen, *duchess*). There's no title above that; someone who's been king twice is just as much of a duke as someone who's reigned a dozen times. (But, if you think that among the ultra-competitive fighter community there's not an informal tally of "who's been king the most," you're fooling yourself.)

People don't really take this whole Crown thing seriously, do they?

At the risk of making an arguably needless introduction needlessly longer, I want to emphasize that whether you're a king or a queen, ruling a kingdom is a great privilege and an awesome responsibility. Nothing in this book is meant to diminish from the respect, authority or honor of any Crown, monarch or kingdom in the Known World. Any tone of familiarity or informality implied in these stories is based purely on the sense of parental affection that I, and I suspect every SCA monarch has for the land and people they rule and serve. The Crown represents the populace, and thus every king and queen deserve royal respect—no one should take this book as license to assume that it's okay to treat a monarch casually, flippantly or disrespectfully.

◆ ◆ ◆

So, there's the FAQ on royalty in the SCA. If it all seems like a whirlwind of titles, jargon and customs tossed around by people who wear funny hats and spend a bit too much time in a make-believe world—well, don't worry, it often seems like that to those of us who sit on the thrones too. You may be a long-time SCA member, or you may only know about the Society through an association with a relative, friend or co-worker, but I suspect you'll find something very familiar in the challenges, obligations and conflicting priorities involved in being a leader or a decision-maker, regardless of whether your title is "Your Majesty," "Mr. President" or "mom and dad."

In truth, the only thing you really need to understand in order to enjoy the "royal escapades" chronicled in this book is the notion that we all see a little bit of our own virtues, struggles and victories reflected in the kings and queens of the SCA. I'm sure you'll find both humor and honor that reflection.

Hey, Ho, the Wind and the Reign
or
Postcards From The Throne, Part 1

I am standing in the restroom at a truck stop just north of Bakersfield wearing a silk *cotehardie* and carrying the Coronet of the Crown Prince. Based on the general condition of this roadside establishment, I would guess that it was built in the early 1920s, before the enactment of several important federal regulations mandating sanitary maintenance of public facilities. Inside the restroom are two discarded tennis shoes (unmatched), a half-eaten McDonald's Happy Meal (in the sink), and the charred remains of a small bonfire (on top of the floor drain). Outside is a truck driver who, by my best estimates, weighs approximately 700 pounds, and who seemed none to happy to be waiting to use the restroom behind a guy wearing a dress.

Welcome to the glory of the Crown…

My regular readers know that my dear, patient, indulgent wife, Felinah and I have recently had the opportunity to reign as King and Queen of Caid. Now that our time on the throne is over, I wanted to share the experience of Royal Life with the many people who, by the very nature of the way we choose our monarchs, may never have a chance to see the view from the Big Chairs. Throughout the reign I kept notes, diaries and outlines so that when the time came, I would be able to describe the experience of ruling the kingdom in a clear, precise and logical manner which would give everybody a bit of insight into the life of SCA royalty.

Yet as I begin sifting through reams of notes, pictures and mementos, I realize that I will be hindered in this task by one tiny, little fact: It's impossible.

Life with the Crown does not proceed in a logical, linear manner. Instead, life becomes a relentless tornado from which the king and queen must pluck the items of greatest importance as they go zipping past, all the while trying to stay in the center of the whirling vortex lest they be blown away themselves. So, throughout this book I'd like to present a series of pieces that can best be described as "Postcards From The Throne"—a somewhat disjointed conglomeration of royal narratives, observances and musings. At times this may seem disorganized, confusing or downright chaotic—please understand that that's exactly what being king and queen is like.

In The Beginning

The evening after Crown Tourney. It is a time for introspection and quiet meditation...for the monks in a secluded Zen monastery somewhere in Tibet, perhaps. For us, however, it is Party Time, and our house is Party Central.

The atmosphere is pure helium. At first, Felinah and I feel like we are floating, and our voices get a little squeaky every time someone addresses us as "Your Royal Highnesses." After a while we start to feel dizzy and a little nauseous. Amidst the hundreds of phone calls, e-mails, handshakes and hugs, we catch each other's eyes from time to time with expressions of increasing panic. What have we gotten ourselves into?

Finally, long after midnight, we go to bed. Notice I did not say "go to sleep." Even I, the poster boy for narcolepsy, spend the next eight hours staring at the ceiling. For Felinah, this night is only the beginning of what is to become one of the most extensive experiments in sleep deprivation in the history of modern science.

Please secure your seatbelts and keep your hands and arms inside the car at all times. Your journey aboard Monarch Mountain is about to begin. It's the wildest ride in the Known World!

Prince Of The Road

Preparing for coronation is like preparing for a wedding. There are clothes to be fitted, gifts to be arranged, ceremonies to be memorized, invitations to be sent...but with a wedding, all this takes place over the course of a many months. There is exactly five weeks to arrange a coronation. Did I mention Felinah wasn't sleeping?

Amidst all of this, I had to take a week-long business trip to South Carolina. Typical of such trips, my work would be completed on Friday, but the flight back wasn't scheduled until Sunday morning as part of a global plot by the travel industry to drive helpless businessmen insane while giving high-powered executives the chance to rack up frequent-flyer miles by sending their flunkies all over the country on their corporate accounts.

So, back when I was nobody, I had made arrangements to spend my unscheduled Saturday at a local tournament in the Barony of Hidden Mountain (Cheraw, S.C.—I'd never heard of it either). Suddenly, however, this was no longer a pleasant little out-of-town visit by some doofus California knight; it had transformed into an inter-kingdom diplomatic incident. The king and queen of Atlantia would be in attendance at the event, as well as the Prince and Princess. And, by the way, a baronial transition was scheduled for opening court—so there would be two sets of barons and baronesses.

The Prince of Caid cannot simply show up with his armor, a sandwich and a folding chair, plop down and say "How y'all doin'?" The Prince of Caid is expected to represent the Kingdom in a manner befitting a Royal Heir. So, the artists of Caid went on Maximum Red Alert to put together a "presentation for eight" worthy of a prince: wood carvings, hand-made game boards, silk banners, jewelry and a lot of other beautiful things started arriving at our house by FedEx almost immediately after word of the trip got out. An old friend of ours, Lady Katherine MacGregor, who now lives in Georgia, took time off of work to make the eight-hour trip to Cheraw in order to attend me in a manner worthy of a Prince. The people of Hidden Mountain arranged breakfast and lunch for me and Lady Katherine, and even furnished an on-site cabin for me to stay in, so that I could be accommodated in a manner worthy of a prince. (No one ever stopped to ask the prince, however, if he felt worthy of the rather intimidating amount of effort and expense being put forth on his behalf.)

The Passing Of The Crown

Meanwhile, Felinah was at home continuing arrangements for coronation. I was getting hourly reports, via cell phone, about the state of our costumes, our fealty tokens, the people who had accepted our invitation to the court and guard, the weather forecast the day of the event, travel itineraries for members of our family who were coming to coronation…did I mention Felinah wasn't sleeping?

I'd love to tell you some funny stories about the weeks leading up to coronation, but I don't really remember most of it. I've got a lot of notes that say things like, "Norman pants! Spandex & leopard spots w/knee trim. Be sure to put this in the book!" I have no idea what these are supposed to mean. I attribute this to a semi-terminal lack of sleep and a diet consisting entirely of espresso and rolled tacos.

So, finally—finally—the day of coronation arrived. Temperature at the site was predicted to be a record high of 104 degrees. We hadn't slept in a week and we hadn't eaten anything except potato chips in two days, but the Crown keeps its own schedule, and does not pause for such human frailties as anxiety or fatigue.

Bleary-eyed and exhausted, Felinah and I came forward to kneel before Edric and Battista and receive the royal mantles. A tremendous amount of work had gone into reaching this moment. We'd called in favors from just about everyone we knew in the SCA, and asked our close friends to do an unbelievable amount of work on our behalf—and we hadn't even officially started the job yet. Could being king and queen really be worth all this effort?

Then, in that pause between the reigns, in that moment when the kingdom is actually without a monarch, Felinah and I stood to face the populace, and I was drawn back to my earliest memories of the Society—back to the days before peerage meetings, procedural handbooks and baronial councils. My mind wandered back to the first time I was inspired by the king's speech on the battlefield at Estrella; to the first time I saw a whole tournament brightened by the queen's smile at opening court. I was reminded that, for the people of the realm, the king and queen personify the honor, grace and nobility of the Current Middle Ages. In that moment, I realized that for the duration of their reign, the king and queen do not just live The Dream, they actually have the opportunity to give The Dream to a new generation.

And that is what makes the terrible privilege and wonderful duty of ruling the kingdom worthwhile. All the filthy truck-stop restrooms visited while rushing to and from events, the sleepless nights, the steady diet of fast-food, and the unending travel preparations seemed to fade away into a sense of sheer happiness and hope in that moment when the whole kingdom echoed with the cheer, "Long live the king!"

To Find the SCA, Just Turn Right at Spiderman

Recently, physicist Stephen Hawking made an announcement that, based on cutting edge research, he has discovered the universe is even stranger and more inexplicable than scientists originally thought. Ironically, this did not come as news to me because I had just spent two days representing the SCA at Comic-Con.

For the six remaining people in the Western Hemisphere who have never been to this event, let me explain. Comic-Con is a convention of some 75,000 comic book enthusiasts, science fiction movie fans, fantasy readers, superhero junkies and war game aficionados who all gather in San Diego once a year for a single purpose: To see ridiculously buxom women dressed in Spandex. At least, that's what I gathered from looking at the artwork, costumes, videos, posters and T-shirts on display at this event.

Although I had never been to a Comic-Con, this year, when our barony announced it would be sponsoring an SCA fighting demo at the convention, I volunteered to help out. I would like to claim this volunteer ethic was completely altruistic, but I must admit there was more to my offer than just a desire to share the Current Middle Ages. I also wanted to see what things were like inside that convention hall—to experience a whole culture dedicated to putting on costumes and pretending to be somebody else for the weekend. There seemed to be something amusing, yet strangely familiar about this concept, so I packed up my armor and headed to the convention center to see what it was all about.

The Comic Fan-Demonium

As soon as I stepped through the front door of the convention center, I realized that this was not going to be your run-of-the-mill SCA demo. In the convention hall, I was surrounded by hordes of stormtroopers, Starfleet officers, Matrix refugees and X-Persons—some of these costumes were being worn by unsupervised 14-year-olds, some were worn by 17-year-olds desperately trying to act like "cool" mature adults (not realizing that "cool" adults rarely point and shriek at the sight of cast members from *Babylon Five*), and some were being worn by 50-year-old professionals acting like unsupervised 14-year-olds. Wearing 70 pounds of armor and carrying a sword and shield through a convention center crowded with hyperactive, over-stimulated sci-fi fans running around with their faces covered by masks and make-up was a little bit like trying to drive an M-1 tank down a crowded New York alley.

As with most conventions, there were lots of high-profile, big-name display booths just inside the doors, and there were plenty of eager fans gathered around to see the attractions. In fact, I think there were so many fans that, in some areas, the oxygen supply was running a little low. At the *Lucasfilm* booth, one of the young Jedi knights (who apparently had not yet learned how to use The Force to cure acne) informed me that his light saber could cut through my armor. At the booth where all of the costumes from *Lord of the Rings* were on display, a gnomeish looking creature informed me that Aragorn's chain mail was much better than mine. At the *Yu-Gi-Oh* booth, a man dressed in a traditional samurai costume with traditional cat ears wanted to take my picture standing next to what I can only describe as a giant ambulatory Hostess Sno-Ball.

But the SCA's booth was not anywhere near these mainstream attractions. If you've ever been to any sort of trade show, you know exactly what I mean when I say our booth was two rows away from the back wall of the convention center—what I mean is: our booth was in the section reserved for the crazy people.

I base this statement on the fact that, to find the SCA booth, you had to walk past the guys selling Spiderman suits for dogs, then turn right at the booth taking orders for custom-molded, latex head tentacles go past the vendor displaying Darth Vader sculptures made of old hardware and car parts and…there we were, the crazy guys who hit each other with sticks.

My first duty at the SCA display was to stand in the aisle and be the "booth attraction." At first I thought Sir Patrick O'Malley, who was organizing the SCA's booth, was crazy for asking me to do this, because the booth next to ours (which was selling 1970s-era plastic Japanese robot toys for prices usually reserved for merchandise measured in *karats*) featured two models signing autographs of their photos in the *Playboy Book of Lingerie*. I assumed there was no way the SCA could compete with that. I quickly realized, however, that at Comic-Con, guys in smelly armor attract a much larger crowd than two scantily clad lingerie models.

At our booth, Sir Patrick had set up a video screen showing footage of the battles from Potrero War. Every time the video depicted a huge, spectacular clash of shield walls, a big "Oooh!" went through the crowd. (Of course, at a normal convention, this would have happened whenever one of the lingerie models in their skin-tight tee-shirts stood up to take a break—but not here.)

When the video was done, I assumed that all of the SCA fighters would field questions about armor and medieval warfare. Instead, the first question I got was: "How do the magic users cast spells in a battle?" I had to explain—repeatedly, in fact—that wizards didn't really exist in the Middle Ages, and that even if they did, their spells were pretty ineffective against a charging band of Viking berserkers. (More than one 15-year-old went away disillusioned after hearing that answer. Several looked like they wanted to whack me with their light sabers.)

Filling Out the Forms

One of the most interesting parts of Comic-Con is the colorful, imaginative costumes worn by the attendees. This is also one of the most dangerous parts of the convention.

At one point I noticed a young woman in a cyborg-style outfit that involved several high-tech, mechanical prosthetics attached to a significantly form-fitting Lycra body suit. Then, just as I was getting ready to make a comment about the form-fittingness of the costume to some of the other fighters loitering near the booth, I realized that the young woman was, in fact, Emma Rose Coe—who, I'm fairly sure, was only 3 years old when I saw her at an SCA tourney the weekend before.

Not long after that, my attention was attracted by another young lady whose entire outfit was constructed out of fishnet stockings that appeared to have been salvaged from an industrial shredder. As this young lady was approaching the SCA booth, her friend, who was wearing some sort of superhero garb, waved at me and said, "Hi, Guillaume!" and I realized that I was talking to Michelle de Sevigny, and that the girl in the fishnet was Loren, the 13-year-old daughter of Duke Armand. I believe that simply by *looking* at Loren wearing that outfit I committed several federal felonies.

After that, I decided to do my best to not notice any more young ladies' costumes at the convention. Perhaps that's why, at one point, I found myself standing right beside a towering female conventioneer dressed in nothing but a latex mini-skirt and a metal corset with two dragon silhouettes strategically cut into the front. Her face was covered in thick Japanese geisha girl make-up and her hair was done in pink and blue spikes. The reason she was towering over me was that she was wearing a pair of 18" platform boots with stiletto heels. She looked at me, I looked at her and we both smiled in a sort of patient, confused way. Then, simultaneously, we both shook our heads and said, "How can you wear that stuff?"

Lost in the Crowd

Finally, the time came to make our way from the SCA booth to the place where we were doing the fighting demo—a walk of hardly more than half a mile or so. Normally, a dozen armored guys clanking through a convention center might have created something of a commotion—but not at Comic-Con.

Instead, I noticed that a huge crowd of people had gathered around a booth selling some sort of DVDs, and everybody was paying little attention to us. They were paying so little attention, in fact, that I had to thread my way very carefully through the throng of hobbits, Vulcans and Bat-beings. As I was passing by, I caught a glimpse of the video they were all clamoring to buy. I assumed it must be something like a pirate pre-release version of the next *Star Wars* movie, but no. I'm not sure I can do justice to what I saw on the television screen in that booth, but I'll try. What I saw was this: 10-year-old girls in plaid skirts and knee socks wielding machine guns and chain saws in a hand-to-hand, martial arts-style melee with an army of bug-eyed slime-covered purple monsters. It seemed to be "The Ninja Catholic School Girls Conquer the Eighth Dimension."

By the time I got through the crowd and reached the place we were going to fight, I realized that nothing we could provide for these people was anywhere near as interesting as what was going on inside.

◆ ◆ ◆

I'll be the first to admit that I went to Comic-Con expecting to find a bunch of hopeless geeks who can't see the difference to between putting on a costume and pretending to be a make-believe fantasy character, and putting on a costume and pretending to be a make-believe medieval knight. I assumed that the SCA, based on action and achievement, would naturally emerge superior to a culture created from media hype and imitation.

But, as so often happens, I found that I'd been wildly incorrect. Everyone I met at the Con was pleasant, kind and genuine. They, like so many of us in the SCA, are intrigued by the complexities of right and wrong, light and darkness and the balances that exist between these ideals. Their heroes may be starship captains or time travelers rather than kings and queens, but the aspirations they pursue and the challenges they face are timeless and universal.

And if there is anyone reading this who has just joined the SCA after watching the demo at Comic-Con, please remember: You won't find light sabers in the *Fighters' Handbook*, and the only spell that is acceptable in this group is "summon coffee" at 7 am on Sunday morning at Pennsic.

A Knight's Castle Is His Home

In the world of the SCA, the pavilion is the primary form of residence. In the Middle Ages, however, only crazed hermits, particularly dim-witted cattle and crusading knights lived in such flimsy structures as pavilions. Sane people, on the other hand, chose to reside in that most famous of medieval structures: the castle.

The castle was a unique symbol of the culture of medieval Europe. And by "culture" I do not mean "socio-political organization"; I mean "rapidly expanding colonies of germs in ideal growing conditions" as evidenced by the fact that most castles were filthy, overcrowded, unheated and infested with rats. Nonetheless, the castle embodied the ruling class of Europe in the Middle Ages—cold, unapproachable and expensive to maintain. It was part palace, part cathedral, part marketplace and part citadel.

Although we do not have any castles at SCA events, we should put forth the scholarly effort and exhaustive research necessary to understand these complex structures that both dominated and supported life in the Middle Ages. This is just the kind of historical insight I would like to provide for my readers in this book; unfortunately, the delivery guy from *Taco Peligro* will be here with my "grandé nacho trough deluxe" in about 10 minutes, so I do not have time to do this. Instead, I will just make some stuff up.

The Real Dirt

The earliest type of castle is known as the *Iron Age hill fort,* because this is a much more polite term than "heaping mound of mud." Early European tribes created these hill forts by digging a semi-circular trench and piling up the resulting dirt along the interior bank of the ditch, resulting in what was, in essence, a speed bump.

One of the finest surviving examples of a hill fort is Maiden Castle in England, so named because, when viewed from above, it looks exactly like a "maiden" would look if she had accidentally fallen into an industrial strength wood chipper. Archeologists now believe this is proof that the builders were influenced by extraterrestrial beings with beer.

Soon—in the sense of "within a period of about 1,563 years"—European warriors began to realize that deterring their enemies by standing atop a dirt mound and hurling rocks, bones, cabbages, shoes and small children was only minimally effective. After much investigation, they began to strengthen these fortresses with the addition of a technological device we have come to call the "pointed stick."

Utilizing this new mechanism, the outer walls of the fortresses were reinforced with vertical wooden ties that were sharpened to a point on the upper end. The addition of these ties allowed the builders to create actual walls rather than just gigantic launching ramps for barbarian invaders traveling at high rates of speed.

The Stench Of Home

The hill fort was only occupied during times of danger; the rest of the time the fortress stood vacant. But the warriors of the early Middle Ages soon began to wonder whether they should continue toiling ceaselessly in the filth and squalor of the farmlands to eke out the barest of livings, or take up residence in their mighty, impenetrable fortresses with all of their swords, lances, armor, horses and men-at-arms to enjoy security and wealth at the expense of the unarmed peasantry. They considered this choice very seriously during the 6.4 seconds it took for the guards to slam the gates shut and bar them with huge logs—and thus was born the medieval castle.

One of the earliest forms of castle was called the *motte and bailey*, named in honor of the famous comedy duo who made their living entertaining medieval troops during long battles. The motte and bailey design consisted of a walled courtyard with a fortified gate on one side and an elevated tower on the other. Developed in France, the motte and bailey was brought to England by the Normans, who began erecting them throughout the southern half of the kingdom with all the restraint of a medieval Wal Mart chain.

Another form of castle utilized during the Middle Ages was called the *donjon*, or *keep*. The donjon was a free-standing, multi-storied square tower containing numerous residential chambers and topped with features called *crenelations*, which were designed to allow defending soldiers to hurl various household items down onto the heads of their attackers without being exposed to missile fire in a rather bizarre medieval form of "hide and seek."

These two basic designs were soon combined into the castles we are familiar with today, consisting of a keep surrounded by a wall with supporting towers and a fortified gate. During times of peace, the lord of the estate would live in the castle, where he would stockpile food, weapons and supplies, host tournaments and celebrations, and plot the overthrow of the king. When the castle was threatened with war, the people of the surrounding area would gather in the protection of the castle bailey where they would live side-by-side with the lord and his knights, defying the enemy soldiers with unwavering resolve until that desperate moment when the peasants actually wanted to eat some of the food they worked so hard to stock in the castle. Then they would be forcibly ejected and left to the mercy of the enemy troops so that the lord and knights of the castle could throw a huge party inside with the remaining wine, bread, cheese and farm animals.

Give & Take

The most dangerous threat to the inhabitants of a medieval castle was the possibility of a *siege*. The word "siege" comes from the Latin "sedere," meaning, "to trap people inside a building until they are so desperate for food that they gladly establish a lucrative market in the sale of live cockroach grubs."

In the Middle Ages, an army would besiege a castle by surrounding it with a force that greatly outnumbered the garrison, resulting in a quiet standoff that could go on for weeks, months or even years. While we might like to imagine medieval warfare as exciting and dramatic, in fact, most military encounters in the Middle Ages were about as action-packed as a corporate tax audit.

Siege warfare was so boring that, after a while, the soldiers began to act in a manner which seems particularly irrational even for people whose skulls had been repeatedly fractured by sword blows. Many historical accounts of sieges claim that the knights inside the castle would call a truce to the hostilities so that they could all put on their armor and come outside the safety of the castle walls and *fight* with the attacking soldiers for sport. (I would like to say that I can't imagine anyone I know doing this, but in fact I know of numerous people, including my lunatic squire Drogo, who would eagerly call a siege "time out" in order to fight a quick tournament on the drawbridge of the castle, even though this would mean they might be accidentally killed by enemy knights, or possibly fall into the moat which had been used as a sewer for several months.)

Apart from death by boredom, there were other ways to attack a medieval castle—all of which seemed to pose the greatest threat to the *attacking* soldiers. The simplest and most stupid method was by direct assault, or *scaling*, wherein the attackers would place rickety ladders against the castle walls and climb up, attempting to dodge the various rocks, darts and kitchen utensils being thrown by the people above. When they reached the top of the ladder, they would be pummeled about the head and shoulders by sweaty, burley men in chain mail with hammers.

Considering the risks involved in a direct assault, the attackers often sought other methods that might prove somewhat less painful to their own personal bodies. In some instances, besieging armies would tunnel beneath the castle walls in order to weaken them so that they would come tumbling down, trapping the miners, crushing everyone in the immediate area and sending the survivors fleeing into neighboring counties.

More commonly, the attackers would attempt to break the walls by hurling huge boulders at them with catapults and trebuchets. These immense, powerful and dangerous machines were typically made of questionably acquired, substandard materials, constructed by drunken engineers with absolutely no safety mechanisms (the weapons, not the engineers) and manned by untrained and frequently belligerent operating crews. As you might expect, these weapons could be expected to work for as many as two or even three shots before malfunctioning and flinging fully armored soldiers several miles downrange, or sending a few hundred pounds of airborne stones in the direction of the commanding general—who was probably one of those unfortunate individuals who had chosen to reside in a pavilion.

The development of military firepower signaled the demise of the castle as well as that of the knight in armor. While miners or siege weapons might batter at a castle for months, a cannon could reduce even the mightiest wall to rubble with just a few shots. Grand and spectacular as well as awesome and intimidating, the castle was, quite literally, the home of chivalry in the Middle Ages. We are fortunate that the SCA gives us a chance to recapture the spirit of romance and glory embodied by the castles of the Middle Ages—without having to put up with the smell of the moat.

Time And Space

"My lords and ladies! Opening court will begin in 10 minutes. Anyone with business before the Crown should speak with the herald immediately!"

"Opening court in *10 minutes!* Geez, the schedule in the kingdom newsletter said opening court was supposed to be held half an hour ago!"

"Well, I heard that the whole tourney is going to be delayed because the autocrat is in the bathroom throwing up after he drank a quart of tequila last night when he heard the feast cook was in the hospital with second degree burns over 40 percent of her body."

"All I know is that if they don't get this fiasco started soon, we'll all be standing around the edge of the field holding flashlights during the final round. Hey, here comes the herald again…"

"My lords and ladies! Opening court will begin in 15 minutes!"

So goes the typical conversation regarding a phenomenon commonly known as *SCA Time*. For those of you who have only been in the Society for a few days and have not had the opportunity to experience this, let me explain: Most tournaments, although scheduled quite rigidly, run "slightly" behind the published agenda. This delay can be as little as 10 or 15 minutes (which will cause people to say, "Hey, I missed court. Are they actually running *on time?*") to as much as a whole *year* late, such as at a baronial anniversary tourney I went to once when the autocrat told me court would be "a little delayed" on account of rain, and which, to the best of my knowledge, has not occurred to this day.

Keeping Time With The Society

Most people complain about SCA time; they feel that if they went to the trouble to haul themselves out of bed at the crack of dawn (8:25 a.m.) on a Saturday, the event should start at the published time, even if that means there's only six people at court—none of them being the king or queen.

While we try hard to give our events the flavor of the Middle Ages, mastery of time is a modern holdover that we choose to ignore; we gripe about SCA time, but very few of us have experienced true *medieval time*.

To understand medieval time, just follow this simple procedure. First, do what you've wanted to do for years and bash your alarm clock with your broadsword. Then, after you've awoken with no clue what time it is, leave your watch behind and don't look at any kind of timepiece all day long. You'll probably wind up confused, disoriented and angry—now you're feeling medieval!

In the modern world, we have watches and clocks to keep us on schedule. In the Middle Ages, however, the primary time-keeping device was the "monk," a marginally dependable instrument which was able, via a complex system of Gregorian chants, to distinguish such accurate times as: time to wake up, the middle of the morning, time to have a beer with lunch, the middle of the afternoon, time to have a beer with dinner, time to have a beer before bed, and "Shut up with the singing, I'm trying to sleep!"

Of course, there were other medieval time-measuring devices, the most common being a time candle. This was a thick candle that burned at a measured rate and had hour notches—it created a clock that, in terms of medieval costs, was similar to allowing your car to idle in the driveway all day if you knew *exactly* how long it would run on a tank of gas. Time candles could also be affected by such small things as undetected air currents causing the wax to melt unevenly, or some boneheaded peasant forgetting to light the wick in the morning. Hourglasses and water clocks were also available to people with lots of money—note, however, that all of these are devices that will *measure* the passage of time, but that's not exactly the same thing as a clock. (It's a little more like trying to tell time with a stopwatch.)

People in the Middle Ages must have been quite relaxed about their schedules (except, of course, for the heralds, who were probably uptight about trivial matters even back then). Undoubtedly the medieval nobles—who, if someone complained about their being late, would either stab them, excommunicate them, or tax them—must have lived by the philosophy, "Everything in its own time."

Here There Be Mappes

While we're on the subject of concepts we take for granted in the modern world, here's another. Flip through the "event announcements" in the latest issue of your kingdom newsletter and count the number of times you read the phrase "map not to scale."

SCA maps and directions are notoriously bad, but even with as much trouble as we have finding SCA tournaments ("I can't read this handwriting. I think we have to turn on Wung Duck Street.") our maps are incredibly accurate compared to their medieval counterparts, which often included such recognizable landmarks as "greate rockkes," dragon's lairs, cloud formations, and restaurants that serve food containing remarkably few rodent hairs.

The medieval concept of direction and travel was very different from ours. Hundreds of things could affect a journey—weather, wars, terrain, poor directions, wars, illness, wars…At 60 m.p.h. on the freeway, we assume we're going to get to our destination in the allotted amount of time, and any little delays, such as traffic jams, road work, or drive-by shootings, are considered aggravating inconveniences. Imagine trying to find an SCA event using a medieval "travelers' map," which is basically nothing more than a straight line with a sequential listing of cities between two points. (At least we know we're supposed to *turn* when we get to Wong Duck Street.)

Folks in the Middle Ages must have had an extremely relaxed attitude about travel, just as they did about time. They certainly never said, "We're going to be 15 minutes late. We'd better think of an excuse!" If someone arrived at a faire, tournament or distant gathering within a week of their plans, they were probably considered extremely punctual.

Certainly time and direction are not the only modern conveniences that we take for granted in the Current Middle Ages. I imagine if the SCA encouraged its members to relinquish modern pharmaceuticals, hygiene, transportation, cuisine, or (God forbid) sunglasses, the group would be much less popular, even if it was more historically accurate.

It's interesting, sometimes, to step back and appreciate our anachronistic mix of the medieval and modern worlds. I'll see you at the next tournament—if I'm running late, feel free to start without me.

Purple Reign
or
Postcards From The Throne, Part 2

By the day of Queen's Champion Tournament—the first official event attended by the new king and queen—we had a firm agenda that we intended to implement throughout our reign. Our goals were: to create an effective network of communication between the baronies, shires and cantons of the kingdom; to facilitate dialogue amongst the kingdom officers in order to advance the financial and administrative goals of Caid; and to oversee the enhancement of the royal regalia so that every monarch would instantly know upon the very sight of the king and queen that Caid was the greatest kingdom ever created in the Known World.

We had nearly completed the first step in implementing this agenda (namely "writing most of it down") when Baroness Luighseach approached the thrones to offer us our first royal breakfast, which consisted of two gigantic cups of coffee and approximately 4,152 warm Krispy Kreme donuts. This breakfast was intended to sustain us during the vigorous activity of placing award medallions around people's necks at opening court, after which our strength was immediately revived by a lunch so large it would probably have sustained the garrison of a sizeable medieval castle for the duration of an extended siege.

This, I'm sure, is all part of a sinister plot on the part of the baronies of Caid to assure that each king and queen become so corpulently overfed that the thrones must be fitted with an annex in order to accommodate the royal derrieres. This plot is carried out when Their Majesties are, at every event, provided with numerous baskets full of authentic medieval delicacies such as cookies, pizza, Hershey's kisses, pistachio nuts, french fries and mocha frappuccinos.

We probably would have started implementing our royal agenda immediately after lunch had we not been delayed by "The Parade of Finals." This occurs when the king and queen must, by ancient and revered custom, personally witness the last round of each and every activity scheduled for the day, including the tournament combat, the fencing competition, the archery, the children's boffer combat, the arts judging, the spelling bee, the sack races, the pie eating contest, the Teen Jeopardy!® tournament of champions, etc.

(Not that watching these finals isn't enjoyable. In fact, the finals of the 6-year-old boffer lists was about the cutest thing we had ever seen. But all of this royal spectating consumes a large portion of the day—sometimes it seemed like "finals watching" began immediately after opening court.)

Once the various finals were complete, we would have launched an immediate implementation of our kingdom agenda had it not been time for closing court. This is where the king and queen have the strenuous task of handing out tabards to all the day's winners. Fortunately, our strength was sustained by a steady supply of ice cream sundaes, fried chicken, sushi, waffles, and what I believe was "deep-fried butter on a stick" provided by our loyal barons and baronesses.

So, by the end of the day we had completely revised our royal agenda from "communicating, facilitating and enhancing" to "trying to fit ourselves into the front seat of our automobile without the use of industrial compression equipment." Perhaps this had something to do with the fact that, later in the week, we felt the deep and sincere royal obligation to trade in our economy car for a full-sized Ford pickup with the optional "maximum payload" suspension package.

King For (More Than) A Day

How do you tell people you work with that you have suddenly achieved the status of "king"? It's a delicate issue, which in my case was compounded by the fact that my co-workers frequently display the tact and social restraint of starving hyenas. So, my idea was simply to say nothing and keep the SCA out of the office.

This strategy worked stunningly well during the approximately 13.7 seconds between when I returned to work after coronation weekend and when someone called my office and asked to speak to "King Guillaume." From then on I was routinely met by co-workers with such greetings as, "I bring thee thy fax, sire," or "When your majesty has a minute, would you be so good as to hand in your expense reports."

So, I learned that whether the king is wearing the Crown or not, it is darned near impossible for him to be anonymous. This phenomenon did, however, give me some very interesting—and at times disturbing—glimpses into the minds of non-SCA people.

The first question on the minds of the hyenas was, "Does the king get to boss people around?" I explained that the populace takes the word of the king very seriously, and that we did have a royal court and guard to help us in our duties.

They didn't quite get the concept, however. For the next few weeks I received a stream of "funny" ideas for various humiliating jokes and abusive tricks I could play on my courtiers, guards and subjects in the name of royal privilege. I tried to explain that when people have sworn fealty and service in exchange for your protection and defense, you don't make them sit on whoopee cushions or eat laxative-laced brownies, but that concept was beyond the hyenas' comprehension. Eventually, they went back to speculating about who was going to get voted off the island on the next episode of *Survivor*, and I went back to hoping that none of them ever runs for public office.

On another occasion, due to the generosity of our subjects, Felinah and I came home with about 70 pounds of chocolate chip cookies. (Actually, *every* weekend we came home with 70 pounds of chocolate chip cookies.) So, because the various assistants and receptionists in my office had been so patient in answering phone calls for "the King," I brought in a plate of these cookies as a way of saying thanks on behalf of the people of Caid.

When I set the cookies down on the lunchroom table, one of the ladies in the office asked who made them. Since the cookies had been part of a larger presentation, I had to answer truthfully that I didn't know exactly who'd made them, but that they had been a gift to us at court.

"Eeeew!" said the woman. "Aren't you worried that they put something in them? I'm not eating them." And, strangely enough, this was pretty much the reaction of everyone in the office—distrust of the generosity of strangers.

In all my time in the SCA I've never heard anyone even joke about showing such disrespect to the Crown. I suppose that in a modern setting, a celebrity or corporate executive would, in fact, have to be suspicious of a gift given by an unknown "admirer," but still…I found the idea that I shouldn't trust the people of my own kingdom downright offensive. At the end of the day I went home with an untouched plate of cookies and diminished opinion of the people in my office.

The Royal Ribbing

I'm sure the members of our court and guard hoped they would be able to be part of a normal reign. I'm sure Felinah hoped she would be remembered as a normal Queen, rather than being part of some bizarre, Salvadore Dali-esque reign that would make the Board of Directors wonder if Caid's status should be changed from "Kingdom" to "lunatic asylum," but all of those hopes gradually faded as our royal tour of duty progressed....

The autocrats of the *Crown Prints Prize Tourney* fundraiser were thrilled to learn that the king and queen would be attending their event. The week before the event, Lady Rowana made the mistake of mentioning to me that she was looking for ideas for the day's raffles, and said the raffle-o-crats would welcome any royal contributions. I'm sure they were hoping for a personal fighting lesson from the king or the chance to write a poem for the queen. From the looks on their faces, I'm sure they were *not* expecting what I offered.

One of the gifts I'd been given at Coronation was a particularly brutal-looking Norman mace—basically an oak slab with about 20 rusty iron spikes driven into the head. Most normal people would have taken one look at this thing and then called OSHA to have the surrounding area cordoned off as a safety hazard. I, however, thought that people (and by "people" I mean "fighters") might pay $1 per ticket for the chance of swinging this mace at a rack of beef ribs hanging from a tree branch.

I cannot even begin to describe the look of horror on the autocrats' collective faces as I told them about this plan. But autocrats are much more reluctant to use the phrase, "Please take your disgusting idea and your dangerous weapon and leave our event," if it has to be followed by the phrase, "Your Majesty." So, after the raffle, the autocratting staff, the spectators, the families in the park having pleasant afternoon picnics, passing motorists and the officers in the police station across the street were all treated to the sight of a grown man assaulting 10 pounds of raw flesh with a three-foot meat tenderizer. When it was all over, the members of our court and guard were treated to the additional experience of wandering around the park picking up sun-ripened fragments of bone and meat from the lawn and surrounding shrubbery as if they'd been hired to clean up after the National Butchers' Union celebratory "beef confetti" parade.

◆   ◆   ◆

Surprisingly, after all of this, no one called for a recount of the blows at Crown Tournament or demanded that the royal pavilion be stocked with Prozac. In fact, we began to see that the more fun we had at an event, the more fun the populace seemed to have as well. At each tournament we felt obliged to put just a little more effort into bringing friendship and merriment to our kingdom—even though that sometimes distracted us from our grandiose plans of completely reorganizing the structure of the SCA.

Most people think the king and queen rule the kingdom—they don't realize that the kingdom also rules the king and queen. The energy, enthusiasm and generosity of the people of Caid inspired us to try to make each tournament, feast or revel more enjoyable than the last. The resulting smiles and laughter were the sweetest gifts we could have received in return—with the possible exception of 70 pounds of chocolate chip cookies.

Why Crown Finals Will Never Be On ESPN

One of the things I spend much of my free time doing (and by "free" I mean "non-SCA" time) is explaining the Society to the people I work with. Several years ago, I was discussing SCA tournaments with a salesman at my place of employment, and I just couldn't get him to understand the Society.

I don't mean he had trouble grasping the concept of the Society itself—I just couldn't get him to understand *why* I found the SCA to be so much fun. Like so many people today, this fellow just couldn't understand why anyone would pursue a lifestyle that offered no potential for success as measured in large quantities of American dollars.

"You don't make *any* money?" he asked, looking at me like I was trying to describe string theory or the new tax laws. I told him that the members of the Society attended SCA events because they enjoy the friendship, the activity and the intellectual challenges involved, but since none of those concepts contained a dollar sign, he just assumed that I was insane and eventually went away.

His question started me thinking, however: Why *don't* we make any money in the SCA? Michael Jordan is rich, Mark McGwire is rich, Doug Flutie is rich, so why don't we see television commercials featuring one of our more prominent dukes eating a bowl of cereal and saying "Before I fight in Crown Prints Prize Tourney, I always eat my Wheaties," or a top-notch knight, surrounded by a roaring crowd, shouting, "I just won crown tournament! Now I'm going to Disneyland!"

It's All In The Marketing

So, why aren't Crown Tourney and Queen's Champion aired on ESPN? Why isn't Estrella called the "Dust Bowl" or the "Known World Series" with 24k gold rings being given to each warrior on the winning army? Such a thing certainly isn't hard to imagine—after all, if millions of viewers will watch grown men drive in a circle at 200 m.p.h. or chase an oblong ball all around a field for three hours, they would certainly be excited by the prospect of watching people beat each other senseless with rattan sticks.

Let's just imagine what an SCA tourney would be like if it was featured on ABC's *Wide World of Sports*. Hmmm...

The herald walks out upon the field, his tabard emblazoned with three Caidan Crescents and the words "Marlboro Lights" and shouts: "My lords and ladies! *Sunday! Sunday! Sunday!* Don't miss the final round of Crown Tournament sponsored by Miller Genuine Draft, Pepsi-Cola, and Nike! After six months of pumping iron and chewing rattan, Count Joseph 'The Battlin' Baron' of Silveroak will meet with the undefeated, two-time King of Caid, Duuuke Patrick! Both knights will grasp for the Crescent Crown, but only one can reign! Crown Tourney XXVII next Sunday only on ABC!"

Then the TV camera would pan across the field to the royal pavilion where the arms of the kingdom on top of the tent would have been replaced with a giant Budweiser emblem, and the cushions on the king's and queen's thrones would be embroidered with the Pennzoil and Burger King logos.

Opening court would have been replaced with a pre-tourney warm-up show sponsored by Easton Sporting Equipment ("Official supplier of Nitro Gel Filled Pole-ARM Gauntlets® to the Calontir army and makers of the new Hott Stikk Jet-Propelled, Computer-Guided Tourney Sword!") in which Janet Jackson would lead a group of 800 fur-clad belly dancers in a fly-girl routine to her new hit single "Chivalry Nation." Then, Vince Gill would come onto the field and lead the crowd in "three cheers" and the national anthem.

With the singing done, the fighters would take the field, each calling out his baronial affiliation ("Sir Ciaran MacDarragh! Barony of Gyldenholt, fighting with broadsword and heater shield. Hi, mom!") and each wearing a tabard with the names and trademarks of various sponsors, from small, local companies trying to establish a name ("Come to Cal Worthington's house of used helms!") to giant mega-corporations marketing new products to the national medieval re-enactment demographic—like McDonalds ("Try our new low-carb haggis"), Secret Roll-On Antiperspirant, ("Strong enough for a knight, but made for a lady,") and Nike Shoes ("Just rule it!").

Finally, as the combat is ready to begin, the marshals cross their staves (encircled with bright yellow Armor-All logos) in front of the cameras, a ripple of tension runs through the crowd as "the wave" goes around the list field...and the station fades to a 20-minute commercial break.

The Joys Of Public Appreciation

Okay, so SCA combat will probably never edge out the NFL or NASCAR racing at the top of the Nielsen Ratings, but it's not hard to imagine a world in which the SCA might have a little more "commercial pizzazz." Not only could the combat be run this way, but so could the Arts Pentathlon, Inter-Kingdom Archery Competitions, and almost everything we do. (Just imagine BoD meetings on C-SPAN!)

There would be a lot of changes, but the basis of all of them would be *money*. With all of those corporate sponsorships, there would suddenly be plenty of cash available for the winners of our major tournaments as well as products donated for the runners up. There would also be salaries available for the autocrats of those events, the expert commentators (Duke Fredrick of Holland could make a fortune doing voice-overs for the instant replays in the finals of Queen's Champion), and other support personnel.

It wouldn't be long before the national membership of the Society would jump to about 4 or 5 million, and suddenly the SCA would be transformed from the friendly, relaxed group it is today to a high-visibility corporate money machine.

Sure, none of us is ever going to get rich in the Society, but at least we don't have to wonder whether this year's woods battle at Pennsic will be delayed by the pre-game entertainment, or redesign our coats of arms at the request of our sponsors to include hamburgers, women in bikinis, or characters from this summer's Disney blockbuster. Perhaps the lesson the SCA has to offer in this regard is that (reality TV aside) there *are* instances where honor and dignity are more valuable than corporate compensation packages—although a field full of Janet Jackson-style belly dancers…well, every rule has it's exceptions.

A Little Touch of SCA in Your Pocket

When you are walking down the street, where do you keep the SCA? Is it in a big cloud all around you, or is it a little memento you keep in your pocket? When you meet a new friend, how long is it before they know about the SCA—15 minutes, or several months? If you asked these questions to 10 people in the Society, you'd probably get 10 different answers.

Almost everyone tries to carry a little bit of the SCA with them in their Monday through Friday, 9-to-5 schedule, but the level of a person's SCA enthusiasm often depends on how long they've been in the group.

I joined the SCA at an age when the major recreational activity of my peers was trying to score 30,000 points on Asteroids (a game that today, I'm pained to say, most teen-agers consider *almost* as antique as cribbage), and when being involved in deviant social activities such as "reading a non-school-required book" could get you stuffed inside your locker for a whole day.

This didn't stop me, of course, from letting everyone within hearing distance know about this great new thing I had found—the SCA—as I sat in the cafeteria assembling my first shirt of mail. I had photos ready to display, I had back issues of the newsletters, I even had membership forms just in case someone wanted to join on the spot.

I didn't even consider the fact that perhaps everyone in the immediate vicinity *didn't* want to hear about the Society until one day the varsity football team captain or first mate or some other type of genetic mutant came over to my table to eat his bananas and asked, "Why are you making armor?" (Or, to be perfectly accurate, he said, "What fer are you makin' that ring-metal thing?")

Suddenly, an image came into my mind: My half-finished mail shirt and I stuffed into an empty locker for the better part of the afternoon until we were rescued by one of the kindly custodians. I wasn't quite sure how to respond, so I simply said:

"Uh…I belong to a club where we dress up in 60 pounds of armor and hit each other in the head. With baseball bats."

He contemplated me for a moment over his side of beef, then said the one phrase which kept me from visiting the inside of that locker:

"You're crazy, dude."

More Of The Same

There have been a lot of years and a lot of tournaments between then and now, and after so many years in the Society, you might think my desk would be surrounded with mounds of SCA mementos, pictures, and *kitsch*. (A Yiddish phrase meaning "useless junk, such as a plastic Hawaiian hula dancer with a clock in her belly, the main function of which is to be dusted.") The average person passing by my desk, however, would have no clue what I did on the weekends. The only visible reminder of my weekend activities is a photo of all of my squires and me on the battlefield taped to my filing cabinet beneath a sign that states: "I don't explain myself—My friends understand and the rest wouldn't believe me anyway."

With that motto in mind, you would think I'd have gathered enough common sense not to shoot off my mouth in the company of strangers, but you'd be wrong.

At a national convention this past January I was talking to one of my business associates who is basically the closest living thing to Indiana Jones there is. He has hunted dangerous big game in Africa, explored the jungles of South America, and opened his own pizza parlor business near a high school where he actually has to watch the courtship rituals of teen-agers. This guy is tough.

We were eating dinner in one of the nicer restaurants in Houston, Texas, (and by "nicer restaurant" I mean "a restaurant which does not permit feed cattle in the dining room"—but that's another story) when this gentleman asked, "What do you do for recreation?"

Several thoughts ran quickly through my head: Do I want this person to think I'm a lunatic? Is he going to think I'm making fun of him? What do I say if he asks if I'm a Satanist, or if I can take a message to Sir Lancelot?

"Well, I'm part of a history club," I said, hoping he would leave it at that.

"Really? What do you do in the club?"

"I wear 60 pounds of armor that took me 10 months to make, and I, uh, hit my friends in the head. With a baseball bat."

Then the man who had canoed up the Amazon and stalked a pride of lions on the plains of Tanzania looked at me over his Gulf shrimp *én brochette* and said:

"Wow. You're crazy."

If the fellow was 20 years younger, he might have looked for an empty locker to stuff me in.

◆   ◆   ◆

Some people are fascinated by stories of the SCA, and some politely wonder if the storyteller has learned to untie the sleeves in the back of his jacket. In either case, I never try to force the SCA on anyone, but never act as though I'm embarrassed by my involvement in the group either. Some of the proudest moments in my life have been in the Society, but, like a new father with a wallet full of baby pictures, I never want to share them without being asked.

My friends understand. Everyone else…well, you know the rest.

Spitting Distance From Chivalry

Many years ago, when I first became a knight, I experienced a great sense of satisfaction in knowing that I had mastered the subtle, yet meaningful virtues of chivalry. This feeling lasted for, I would estimate, three minutes. Then, I realized that striving for the knightly virtues is a difficult task for anybody, from a respected peer to the newest member of the Society, and sometimes the most powerful lessons in chivalry come in very unexpected moments.

For instance, two years ago, Felinah and I traveled to the town of Mt. Shasta in Northern California (where most of her family lives) to celebrate the Fourth of July. Mt. Shasta is one of the top five places in America to celebrate this holiday, as measured in gross tonnage of fireworks for sale on any given street corner. Last year Felinah's brother, John, and I liquidated our respective retirement accounts in order to purchase every explosive item and pyrotechnic device within several hundred square miles of the town—including something which, to this day, I believe was a half-used box of Kleenex with a fuse at one end.

Mt. Shasta is also a great place to enjoy another tradition: the Fourth of July parade. Every year the city hosts a parade which features everything you could expect from a small-town festival: the city mayor riding on a float pulled by a logging truck, the Jr. High School cheerleading squad performing tumbling routines with bare hands and exposed knees on asphalt which is hot enough to melt tennis shoe soles, and six red-neck grease monkeys crammed into a "tricked '63 Camero" which, over the course of the half-mile parade route, consumes 17 gallons of gas, burns three quarts of motor oil and emits a cloud of black smoke which can be seen from the Oregon border.

The homespun atmosphere of the parade makes it very popular, and anyone who does not wish to watch it from somewhere on the planet Neptune has to arrive early to reserve a viewing area by arranging folding chairs, ice chests, traffic cones, patio furniture, gardening equipment and small dogs into a "defensive perimeter." Last year, Felinah's 17-year-old niece, Megan, and I were given the job of staking out the family's parade-watching spot because the two of us had expressed an interest in "getting a totally awesome seat for the cool parade," as well as "finding a decent cup of coffee in this backwater town since you all insist on waking up at this ungodly hour." (Actually, these were our two individual, respective goals, but since they coincided nicely, we decided to share the task.)

And that was how Megan and I came to be on the sidewalk of Main Street to witness the event which kicks off the whole Fourth of July celebration: a five-mile fun run. The starter's pistol was fired as the two of us were setting out enough lawn chairs to accommodate the Boston Philharmonic Orchestra, and as the runners began scrambling over the starting line, Megan said, "That looks like fun."

Then I, probably due to the fact that the only coffee house in Mt. Shasta was not yet open, mumbled, "Yeah, it does. Maybe we should try it next year."

Megan's face lit up with the kind of smile that only a 17-year-old has the energy and enthusiasm to produce. "Really? That would be totally awesome! Yeah! Let's do it."

I nodded a bit, not realizing what kind of trouble I'd gotten myself into, and went to see if I could find any old coffee grounds in the trash can behind a nearby sidewalk café.

Exercises In Futility

Soon, the parade started—the parade of time, that is. Summer turned to autumn, which turned to winter, and then to spring again. Before I knew it, summer was on the horizon once more, and Felinah and I were again making plans to visit Mt. Shasta for the Fourth of July.

One day, somewhere around the middle of May, Felinah told me, "My brother called earlier. He said Megan is really looking forward to going on that run with you this year."

Unfortunately, there were two tiny things that, at this point, were standing in the way of Megan and I successfully completing the Fourth of July run. The first was the fact that Megan was one of the star runners on her college track team; the second was the fact that my idea of strenuous physical activity was walking into *Javier's Cubo de Carnitas Manteca* instead of using the drive-thru window.

Besides, I rationalized to myself, I have Very Important Business to attend to, and I cannot be bothered with meaningless little things like a small-town fun run. So, I resolved that I would politely back out of my commitment to go running with Megan by explaining to her that I had many other obligations, such as...well, I was sure I had some somewhere that did not involve playing "Quake 3" on-line, and as soon as I figured out what they were, I'd call and explain them to her, and she would understand why I, as an important, respected, professional, executive-type adult, had to break our informal little pact.

For a few days, I let this dilemma rattle around in the back of my mind as I awaited a revelation from the heavens that would show me a graceful way to deal with the situation. I didn't have to wait long, although the revelation wasn't exactly what I expected.

I was having lunch with my boss one afternoon and, just as a way of making small talk, I told him about my predicament. With typical boss-like compassion, he snorted through a mouthful of Thai noodles and said, "Don't make such a fuss over some silly promise. She's just a kid. Blow her off—she'll get over it."

And, as my boss went back to slurping up his noodles and talking about semi-inverted gross distribution channels, or something like that, I discovered he had just given me a lesson in chivalry which could only have come from a Zen monk or a total jerk. I realized that I didn't want that girl with the bright smile and the unabashed, youthful enthusiasm to have to "get over it." Inspired by my boss' philosophy, I went home that evening, excavated my jogging shoes from the back of the closet and made a resolution to at least *attempt* to get into condition for the run.

There were a few sore muscles and stiff joints at first, but I found I wasn't quite as out-of-shape as I'd feared. I established a two-mile route through the neighborhood, and every day I increased the distance by a block or two. By the beginning of July, I was running four and three-quarter miles every afternoon, and I resolved to finish the last quarter mile on the day of the race by sheer determination, even if it killed me.

At 7 a.m. on the Fourth of July, Megan and I were at the starting line of the five-mile run, just as we'd promised. I did a pretty respectable job of challenging Megan's running ability—or, perhaps, Megan did a good job of making me feel like I could win a spot on the college track team at age 36 when, in fact, that five-mile race was barely a warm-up for her. Nonetheless, we had a great time, and after we crossed the finish line, we sat in the shade beside the hardware store on Main Street where Megan taught me the proper college track team method of "hocking up a post-race loogie." I felt the satisfaction of knowing that this girl's memory of her Uncle Guillaume would include laughing and sweating and spitting into a vacant lot, but would *not* include "getting over it."

Chivalry is comprised of many aspects, and one of the most important is faith—honesty, dependability and integrity. In the modern world, we're often expected (if not openly encouraged) to wriggle out of inconvenient commitments rather than investing the time and effort necessary to honor our promises. As we follow the code of chivalry in the Current Middle Ages, it's worth remembering that the virtuous tenets of that code can, and should, stay with us in our modern lives as well—at least, if you want to be the kind of person with a reputation for faithfulness and trust, instead of one who is sometimes mistaken for a Zen monk.

Chronicles of the Inquisitor, Part 1

I need to begin this chapter with an explanation. During our reign, several strange, bizarre, amusing incidents occurred rather spontaneously—in fact, you might say the entire reign was made up of such incidents. While these incidents had very little to do with the formalities of being on the throne, they were, as we say in the world of journalism, "too good to pass up." Thus, after the end of the reign, I asked someone called "The Inquisitor"—a shadowy, retiring entity with a nearly omniscient awareness who, nevertheless, chooses to reside in the coat closet in our guest bedroom—to set down his recollections of these incidents in writing, just as the great medieval chroniclers such as Matthew Paris or Geoffrey de Villehardouin would surely have done had they run out of real news to cover.

So, with that in mind, here's the first of a three-part series called "Chronicles of the Inquisitor," that details events that took place (thankfully) outside the public eye during our reign.

♦　　♦　　♦

The first incident that I must relate to you occurred at a meeting of the revered Order of the Laurel, which Guillaume, being king, was allowed to attend. The order's appreciation of his presence was expressed by the first item of business that Mistress Angelina, secretary of the order, had put on the agenda: "Debate regarding whether or not to duct tape king's mouth shut."

Fortunately, royal participation in the meeting turned out to be a very minor issue. Guillaume, with his considerable attention span, was captivated by the intellectual discussion of the arts and sciences for almost 13 full seconds. After that, he began to search for something to amuse himself with which involved either breaking furniture or setting something on fire.

Glancing around the room, Guillaume saw that a party held in the home of the meeting host had resulted in several unused piñatas being strewn around the room. One of these piñatas was shaped like the animated dog "Blue" from the cartoon *Blue's Clues*. As the Laurels' discussion of the arts and sciences continued, Guillaume felt that he could add to the order's body of knowledge by quietly demonstrating that Blue was hollow and that the king's entire hand could fit inside Blue's head.

At nearly the same time, Guillaume also spotted another "leftover" item from the previous night's party: a six-pack of Silly String aerosol spray cans. It was not long, therefore, before Guillaume in his finite royal wisdom put these two pieces of data together by placing an entire can of Silly String inside Blue's head.

At this point, the meeting reached a lull and the members of the order turned to the king to ask whether it would be the royal pleasure to continue with the next item of business, or to take a short refreshment break. Guillaume looked at them all momentarily with an expression of great compassion, then held up the piñata and said, "I think we should take a break, 'cuz Blue's allergies are bothering him. Tell us how you feel Blue."

Then he made an appalling "Ah-choo!" sound and sprayed green Silly String out of the piñata's nose, striking members of the Order of the Laurel who were sitting as far as 20 feet away.

This joke was met with the uproarious sound of horrified silence, so Guillaume repeated it several times just in case anyone had not fully appreciated the subtle humor of their king causing slimy green string to shoot out of the nose of a *papier-mâché* dog.

The Laurels' appreciation of this prank was so great that in less than a minute Mistress Angelina was considering whether a simple majority vote would be sufficient to add "beat king to death" to the agenda. Fortunately Mistress Maria Theresa devised a more expedient way of calling for a recess by acquiring her own can of Silly String and conducting an experiment (remember: it's arts *and* sciences) to determine whether string sprayed into the king's right ear would, in fact, shoot out through his left ear.

Just for the record: It did not.

This is a true and accurate account of the events that transpired upon the said day, as I witnessed them. Whether these events were merely the actions of fallible mortals, or divinely inspired, I cannot say, for the ways of gods and kings are strange. Very strange.

By my hand,
The Inquisitor
To Be Continued…

Comments From The Red Belt Gallery

Dear Readers:

A bit of backstory is necessary before reading this chapter. Several years ago, Guillaume took part in a demonstration of Newton's first law of motion involving a high-performance racing snowmobile and a fast-moving Douglas fir tree. The resulting broken arm and dislocated wrist reduced Guillaume's level of proficiency on the "electronic scribe" from 70 words-per-minute to being able to operate the space bar with the big toe of his left foot if he tried really hard.

Thus, this chapter is the result of Guillaume's posse of squires graciously volunteering to cheer him up during his time of "keyboard invalidity" by composing their own short writings, all inspired by the teachings of their knight, which they hoped would be entertaining, and at the same time would motivate Guillaume to get back to writing his own stories as quickly as possible.

—*The editor*

Norman Contributions To Western Civilization

By Lady Alix de Beaumont

As you probably know, Sir Guillaume is a member of the species known as "Normans," a swaggering, self-aggrandizing, bombastic people who, in 911 A.D., settled northwestern France in roughly the same gentle, placid manner as it was "settled" by American and British commandos on June 6, 1944. Guillaume has made an effort to inform his squires—and indeed everyone in the Known World—that Western society would never have reached its current state of enlightenment if not for the Normans. Here then, are a few of the most important cultural contributions of those hearty Normans according to our knight:

• The Jury System—Prior to the coming of the Normans, legal disputes were settled by an old Danish custom involving dice and axes. The Anglo-Norman king Henry II, however, created a new system whereby two individuals could present their cases before "twelve good men and true" who would listen for hours to arguments, claims, counter-arguments, tortes, counter-claims, and the ever-popular rebuttals, until finally they gathered in a little room to vote on which of the two adjudicants they were going to beat to death. The strength of the Norman jury system survives to this day, as demonstrated by the revered legal axiom: "If le glove don't fit, ye must acquit."

• Agriculture—Early in the Middle Ages, agricultural technology was pretty much limited to three steps: "poke hole in mud, plant seed, starve." Seeing the need for innovation, Norman knights selflessly aided the process by gathering huge numbers of soldiers mounted on massive war horses to indiscriminately rip up acres of farmland by holding battles on them. This gave the peasant farmers the impetus needed to create such innovations as fallow fields, quick-growing strains of wheat, and the longbow.

• The Lexus—Normans were the first people to create the concept of "luxury transportation that low-lifes like yourself have no hope of ever affording." A trained Norman destrier might be worth as much as an entire barony, while the broken-down, disease-infested beast of burden used by a peasant family would be roughly equivalent in value to the crud that a Norman knight could pick from under three or four of his fingernails.

• Cuisine—While the rest of the medieval world was eating what we might now consider "shoeleather," the Normans were inventing the culinary concepts of cheese sauce, prime rib, Brie, herb-flavored butter, heavy cream and coronary artery disease. Wherever they went, the Normans combined their cuisine with local dishes to create new and dynamic tastes. When people in Normandy started eating snails, however, the Normans gave Normandy back to the French.

• Tournaments—Only a knight—and I say this after years of experiencing the deep, inner workings of Guillaume's mind—could come up with the concept of attacking your friends and neighbors with razor sharp swords and spears as a form of recreation. It took the Normans, however, to devise a system wherein you could make money at it.

A Knightly Guide To Authentic Art

By Drogo FitzWilliam (once squire, now "sir")

To be a knight—which, of course, all good squires aspire to be—is to be more than just a head-thumping, knee-brace-wearing, non-gambeson-washing, holding-the-challenge-field-until-several-hours-after-dark sword jockey. A knight (as my knight has taught me) must have a thorough understanding of the arts, crafts and sciences of the Middle Ages and a mastery of that most medieval artistic medium: duct tape.

I was first taught the artistic merit of duct tape at the fighter practice after I was squired to Sir Guillaume. There, Guillaume gave me a 45-minute lecture on the correct method to put tape on a stick of rattan. The under-layer of nylon filament tape, Guillaume says, must be wrapped spirally—not lengthwise—and there must be *four* layers of it over the front half of the sword, but only *two* layers of it over the back. Then, the duct tape must be carefully applied lengthwise—not spirally—and if you are unable to crease it into perfect hospital corners as it bends over the tip of the sword, you must remove it and start again. I'm not even going to get into the subtleties of color choice and application of the edge-marking tape. (Bear in mind, all of this is going onto a stick which, approximately 34 seconds after it is put to use, will look as though it has served as a pull toy for a pack of hyperactive Rottweilers who are fed a steady diet of Starbucks coffee.)

Over the years Guillaume has shown me that duct tape is, in fact, a staple of medieval art. For example, once, as part of a tournament contest, Guillaume made an entire pig (no, I am not kidding) out of nothing but a roll of duct tape, a coat hanger and about as much foam rubber as you would need to fill Dodger stadium to a depth of 40 feet. And the most amazing part is, apart from being bright silver, it was perhaps the most life-like pig I've ever seen outside of a taxidermy shop.

After many years, I, too, have come to understand the artistic value of duct tape. In order to honor my knight, at the last *pas d'arms* in Calafia I created an elaborate crest for my helm using that most authentic of medieval artistic materials. Calling upon the lessons Guillaume had taught me, I duct-taped a roll of toilet paper to the top of my helm. I expected my knight to tell me to remove it before the fighting began, but, in fact, he complimented me on how nice it looked and even took a picture of it later in the day. (I'm not sure he ever realized exactly what it was.)

So, young fighters, you see that the quest toward knighthood would be incomplete without a proper appreciation of medieval art. Be sure to pick up an extra roll of art next time you're in the hardware store.

MacNebbish Hae Goon To Th' Highlands

By Laird William Jakes, Scotsman & Kiltwearer
    Lough! Lough sae the clansmen
    Whae the sassanach, skirge a' th' sooth,

Bates tae rouin Clan MacNebbish
Aen tae aur bonnie sheep awaie!
Skirl the pipe and hoon the drum,
Oon fling th' mud ta din their mail,
Noo we'll ne'er nee a noomen…

Editor's note—*Although this spirited Scottish ditty continues for several more pages with frenzied, semi-incoherent accounts of various highlanders being bravely beheaded, disemboweled and tortured, let us "cut to the chase" as they say in the highlands, and bring this poem to its logical (and typical) conclusion:*

Ach, me bonnie highlands, I'll ne'er see ye more,
It's auf to Canada fer me! Tewdles!

The Colorful Lights Of The Middle Ages

By Lady Jeanne-Marie la Verriere

When I first discovered the SCA, I was awed by its many activities: dancing, fighting, feasting, singing, costumes, cooking…I wanted to try them all! But at every event I saw all the people who had been doing these things for many years, and I was afraid I'd never fit in, or that no matter how hard I tried I'd never be as good as those people whose work I admired.

As I came to more tourneys and wars, however, I began to learn (with a little advice from my knight, Sir Guillaume) that the people in the SCA are like those beautiful stained glass windows in the medieval cathedrals. Each piece has a hue and a shape all its own. Individually, each bit of glass is really nothing more than a scrap, but when you put several together, you see that the odd and broken pieces fit into places that no other piece will, and that the bright colors of some are made even more beautiful when complimented by the subtle shades of others. And, bit by bit, all those shards eventually become a glorious work of art.

Each of us—from squire to knight to Their Most Regal Majesties—fits into a place in the beautiful window of the SCA. I'm glad that with the company of my friends, my family and my knight (a piece of the window which now has a few extra cracks) I'll be able to be a part of the luminous world of the Current Middle Ages for a long time to come.

Of Arms and the Knight I Sing

Phase I: Stupidity

Riding along through the snow with the wind in my face, 20 miles away from the nearest automobile or telephone, I began to imagine I was a medieval knight out on a sleigh ride, bundled up in a heavy cloak, gliding through an icy forest, knowing that a blazing hearth was waiting for me on my return to the castle...

Unfortunately, there were a few problems with my little winter fantasy, as I steered my snowmobile down a frozen hillside in Idaho last December.

First, a medieval knight would not have been out in weather approaching 40 below zero because he would not have had a GoreTex parka and battery-powered, heated gloves to keep him from freezing to death. He would have been at home, in front of his blazing hearth, whipping his servants for neglecting to put enough cloves into his hot mulled wine.

Second, a medieval knight would have been riding on a sedate, horse-drawn sleigh, not a neon green, high-performance snowmobile powered by a 1,000 cc racing engine capable of 0 to 60 mph acceleration in under 4 seconds.

Third, and perhaps most important, while daydreaming about a medieval sleigh ride, I had neglected to notice that the inside of the Lexan visor on my helmet had frozen into a solid sheet of ice, thus preventing me from seeing that I was headed directly toward a 40-foot fallen log which had cleverly camouflaged itself with a coating of approximately .03" of snow.

A moment later the tinny buzz of my snowmobile's engine was replaced by the sound of crunching plastic and aluminum, followed almost instantly by the sound of wind rushing past my head as I flew through the air and the staccato rhythm of snowmobile parts hitting the ground all around me.

When I finally plopped down into a snow bank, my first thought was, "Well, that wasn't as bad as standing up to a Drafn shield charge. Heck, I didn't even get a scratch." Then I stood up and brushed away the snow...and I noticed my left hand was sort of twisted around at a 45-degree angle and pointing off to the side like I was trying to hail a taxi in a Salvador Dali painting. Fortunately, just at this time Felinah, who was riding her own snowmobile, drove up and—drawing upon years of medical training and diagnostic experience—said, "Um, you don't look so good."

Phase II: Immobility

Six hours later, I was in the surgical recovery ward of Rexburg County Hospital. There were two pins in my arm holding together the various hunks of bone that formerly were my wrist, and my left arm was encased in fiberglass and nylon.

Lying there, half-dazed on medication which I'm sure was originally developed for livestock use, I began to wonder what would have happened to a real medieval knight with a similar injury after taking a bad fall from his horse during a battle or tourney. Contrary to popular opinion, not all doctors in the Middle Ages were ignorant butchers. A wealthy duke or baron would likely have enlisted the services of a physician who'd studied anatomy in Italy and seen surgical procedures performed by doctors trained in Greece or Persia. For a loud-mouthed Belgian knight who had insulted the king once too often, however, medical care would probably have come in the form of a country hack who studied anatomy behind the barn with Geraldine the milkmaid, and whose training in surgical technique consisted of helping his father cut fence posts with an axe.

I imagined a crippled knight, trying to survive one-handed without any discernable job skills other than the ability to whack people with a sword. I imagined a once-great warrior reduced to relying on the generosity of friends and relatives, or perhaps begging in the street for his meals.

Then I began to imagine how, exactly, I was going to put on a pair of pants with only one arm.

Phase III: Recovery

I soon realized that living with an injury—even a relatively minor injury—isn't simple. When the doctor released me from the hospital, he mentioned that the pins in my arm might cause slight discomfort during certain types of motion. What he failed to explain, however, was that "certain types of motion" meant the "motion of the earth revolving around the sun," and that "slight discomfort" meant "jagged red-hot bolts of pain shooting up my arm like someone was pulling on the pins with a pair of Vise Grip-brand pliers."

The doctor told me to expect my arm to be sore and tired; he did not tell me that I was going to have to wear a trash bag in order to take a shower, or that I was going to have to perform *Cirque du Soleil*-style contortions in order to get my shoes tied, or that I was going to wake myself up about 36 times every night by rolling over and clubbing myself in the head with two pounds of resin-impregnated fiberglass. All of these things I discovered by myself as with each passing day my broken arm, and the resulting lack of self-reliance, weighed on me more and more.

Two weeks after the crash I went to a Twelfth Night dinner hosted by the House of the Five Belles. Normally, I would have pulled up to the driveway and, in the time of about two minutes, slipped into a tunic, slid on my boots, set my coronet on my head and trotted inside to enjoy a wonderful meal.

With only one arm, however, putting on a tunic became a struggle—the sleeve was just barely big enough to let my cast slip through, and once on, was too tight to allow me to move my left arm at all. I got my right boot on with a moderate amount of struggling, but my left boot just wouldn't cooperate, so I stumbled around looking for something to push my foot against. Meanwhile, I was trying to loop three feet of leather through my belt buckle with one hand while simultaneously steadying my coronet with the elbow of my cast.

At this point Baron Thorvald walked up, looking regal and dignified in his full noble splendor, to find me with one boot on and my belt around my ankles, waving both arms in the air trying to catch my coronet. "Do you want some help?" he asked.

I am not accustomed to needing help. I am used to being the big, strong fighter who can carry ladies' baskets and set up the baronial pavilion and bend steel with my bare head. I didn't like relying on other people to put on my clothes, pour my water, cut my food, or do any of the other little minor tasks that I just couldn't do one-handed. The things that I had once found very enjoyable—like going to SCA events, making armor, writing and gardening—became unpleasant burdens. I found myself becoming more content to just sit and watch TV.

Phase IV: Stupidity (You Didn't Think The Doctor Cured That, Did You?)

After five weeks, the time had finally come for the pins to be removed from my wrist. Needless to say, I was a bit surprised to learn that the precision surgical instrument used to perform this task would be: a pair of Vise Grip-brand pliers. Fortunately, with the pins removed, the doctor replaced my full arm cast with a much shorter wrist cast. He told me that the pains in my arm would rapidly subside, and that I could participate in just about any moderately strenuous physical activity.

So, after a few minutes of convincing Felinah that being beaten with a yard of rattan qualified as "moderately strenuous," I dusted off my armor and headed to fighter practice. For the benefit of those fighters reading who may someday feel an insane need to fight with a cast on their arm, let me explain the benefits and drawbacks.

On the positive side, a half-inch of solid fiberglass is about the best armor you could ask for. Even though I put my vambrace and gauntlet over my cast, there was really no need. Nothing short of pneumatic concrete demolition equipment could have damaged my arm.

Unfortunately, I discovered the negative aspect of putting armor over a cast later that evening when I went to bed. I turned off the lights, pulled up the blankets and curled up next to my lady. I was just starting to relax when I heard her sniff softly once or twice, then ask, "Honey, did you take a shower before you came to bed?"

My cast, being essentially nothing but a nylon and cotton batting sandwich, had an extraordinary ability to retain odors, and as I lay there in bed it was emitting the distinctive stench of half-rotten leather, rusted steel and fighter sweat.

To me, however, it was the smell of freedom.

Phase IV: Needless Analysis

A few weeks and several fighter practices later, I was at the Unbelted Tourney trying to keep my cast downwind of the royal pavilion. As I was watching the fighting, Sir Alberic Reed approached me and asked how I was doing. I launched into a long discussion of my "near-death" experience and the life-changing revelations I'd had in the weeks that followed. After listening to me drone on for about 20 minutes, Alberic, with a certain degree of patience, wisdom and insight that only one of the senior members of the Order of Chivalry can display, said: "What on earth is wrong with you, boy? It's just a cast. Get over it."

For seven weeks I had the opportunity to demonstrate the triumph of the human spirit over adversity, and I stumbled at every hurdle I came to. The only lasting impressions that remain from my accident are three small scars on my wrist and a tremendous admiration for those people who must cope with a physical disability of some kind at every tourney, every feast, every war and every day of their lives. They face their challenges with a sense of grace, honor and courage that I can only dream of—and, now that I have both hands back in working order, I am glad that I can applaud their courage and fortitude.

Fortunately, we live in a Middle Ages where disability does not mean defeat, where the physically challenged are welcomed with respect and dignity, and where a gimpy, grumpy old knight can come with one arm in a sling and not have to beg for his dinner. May we never forget just how lucky each of us is who can lightly take up a sword, or a quill, or a lute and pursue our chosen form of recreation free from any disability other than our own lack of talent—and may we never bypass the opportunity to lend a hand, a healthy, working hand, to individuals who don't have that luxury.

The Reign At Pennsic Falls Mainly On The Plain
or
Postcards From The Throne, Part 3

We were nearly half-way through our reign ("Three months? Already? It can't be!!!") when the time came to make the journey to Pennsic. For two weeks before departure we spent our evenings filling boxes with royal regalia and sending them off via UPS (Of course UPS delivers to Pennsic!) so that we would be able to represent our kingdom in a style as grand and regal as two people possibly can when living out of nothing but carry-on luggage for seven days.

We arrived at Pennsic with an appointment book full of royal luncheons, queen's teas, state dinners, and "can't be missed" activities. Lady Ceridwen, our chief attendant and "handler" for the week, immediately began setting up a contact station where members of the court and guard could sign in, messengers could leave correspondence and our current position could be tracked by Doppler radar 24 hours a day. Because, of course, the king and queen cannot be without attendants, and nowhere is this more true than at Pennsic

Don't get me wrong—this is a good policy. When you're surrounded by 11,000 people, this allows the populace of each kingdom to show their respect for the dignity and authority of the Crowns of the Known World. But as a monarch, maintaining that level of dignity and authority for seven full days is somewhat of a challenge when you're being followed by a royal procession, complete with a herald and the kingdom banner, on a trip to the food court for a cup of coffee. Or when you're in a port-a-potti with two armed guards outside the door.

The Pennsic Royal Team

The first of the obligatory royal events was the formal Declaration of War, which took place on the first day of Pennsic. Don't let the phrase "first day" fool you, however—by this point, people had been "setting up" for more than two weeks. Some camps included full-sized Tudor houses and functional castle drawbridges. One had a Doric Greek temple with a mosaic-tile floor set into the earth. Our own camp, which had been assembled by Baron Bartholomew's carpentry crew, included a 12' blue-and-white crescent gateway and a border of hanging lanterns—and it was positively Spartan by comparison.

Fortunately, Lord Lancetta was on hand to make sure the king and queen did not look shabby in the procession department. The Declaration of War was the first chance each of the kingdoms had to measure one another in terms of unabashed royal opulence. In years past, some monarchs have ridden into the ceremony on horseback; some marched in with their armies; some were preceded by dancers, jugglers and fire-eaters.

We entered in a rickshaw.

I'm not sure how, exactly, Lancetta fit it into his carry-on luggage, but he provided us with a working rickshaw, complete with canopy and shock-absorbing chassis. To top it off, our "draft team" was led by none other than Lord Rowan, the kingdom seneschal—who spent the rest of the week telling seneschals of other kingdoms, "Hey, you think *your* king is demanding…?" As we rolled into the ceremony, flanked by armed guards and heralded by Master Giles, the other kings' and queens' eyes got a little wider, a murmur ran through the audience, and we knew we had just aced our first test at Pennsic. For the rest of the day, at least, we were gods among royalty.

Caidans In Hell

Monday evening—our first night at Pennsic—when all of our official royal duties were complete, we decided to tour the camp and see some of the legendary Pennsic nightlife. We were only lightly attended, since many of Her Majesty's guard had retired early so they'd be well rested for the opening battle the next morning.

So, accompanied only by Hrodrnavar, Rowan and Ceridwen, we went for a walk around the lake. We were admiring the many beautiful campsites amidst the streams and woods, when up in the distance, a pulsing, glowing object caught our attention. As we neared, we saw that this was, in fact, a 20' tall, cast iron, pro-

The Reign At Pennsic Falls Mainly On The Plain or Postcards From The Throne, Part 3

pane-powered sign which read, in giant, spewing letters of flame: "Welcome To Hell."

Beneath, in a fenced courtyard, we saw hundreds—perhaps thousands—of people, shoulder-to-shoulder, in various stages of dress, some of them locked into stocks, some being flogged by women in bustiers and net stockings (and seeming to enjoy it), all drinking out of glowing red, smoking tankards in what looked like a cross between a Hieronymus Bosch painting and a scene from Termintor 2.

As we stood there, peering through the gate, I heard a rather sheepish voice nearby: "Uh, hello, Your Majesty."

And I turned to see Lord Andrés, stripped to the waist and soaking wet, accompanied by Lady Ciana, Lord Jonathan Whitehart, and the rest of the members of our queen's guard. Apparently, "getting rested for tomorrow's battle" included taking part in an activity called "Bobbing For Bourbon." Of course, they tried to offer several feeble excuses for their behavior—"My baldric fell off and was blown in here," "We heard Marcel was being held captive, and we came to rescue him," "We were challenged by the Meridian queen's guard to a bourbon bob-off" etc.—but we quickly discovered the real culprit. Slinking off into the shadows was none other than Sir Alaric, the queen's champion, who had been responsible for luring the entire guard into the party.

So, with the help of the Polite Dungeon Master, who stopped by just at that moment to serve us steaming drinks, we sentenced Andrés and Alaric to be placed in stocks and flogged by scantily clad young women and fed glowing red bourbon until they begged for mercy. Neither of them seemed to object too much as they were led away—I'm sure they knew, deep down in their hearts, that they deserved the punishment they'd received.

Courting Disaster

Another of the obligatory activities for every monarch at Pennsic is to hold a Royal Court. We chose to host ours in one of the community pavilions near the Greek restaurant with a fountain in the dining room. (Of course they have restaurants with fountains inside at Pennsic!)

We didn't really have a lot of "business"—we expected this to be just an excuse for everyone from Caid to enjoy dinner together, and for us to officially thank everyone for making the trip with us. But, as so often seemed to happen in our reign, things at court kinda got out of control.

First, a few former Caidans stopped by with greetings from distant lands. Then, several minstrels and bards came to entertain in honor of new Caidan friends they'd made during the war.

Finally, the herald called forward Luqman and Julianna, the baron and baroness of Hidden Mountain. This was the barony—for those of you who don't hang upon every word written in this book—which I visited as crown prince, and Luqman and Julianna had shown me great hospitality.

So, when Their Excellencies heard we were holding court, they came by to say hello. They shared their warm smiles with all of our assembled subjects, then they gave us a nice little presentation—candy, goblets, and a pair of matched, His Majesty and Her Majesty Super-Soaker squirt guns. (I don't really know *why* these were a part of the presentation. I guess they just felt like every California King needs a good squirt gun.)

Unfortunately, Their Excellencies showed the extremely poor judgment to present these squirt guns to us loaded, charged and ready to go. Seeing this, I felt that these fine weapons needed to be given an immediate test firing, and Lord Andrés, perhaps still feeling somewhat penitent after the Hell party incident, leapt up and presented himself as a target.

So, always quick to take advantage of such a situation, I raised my squirt gun, took aim and...

"We thank you for this gift," interrupted Her Majesty. "We also thank you for taking such good care of Guillaume while he was visiting your barony in Atlantia."

"Yeah," I said, in a royal demeanor, then lifted my squirt gun, took aim, and...

"Also," Felinah continued, "We would be honored if you would join us for dinner here at our court, so that we can show our gratitude and friendship."

"That'd be great," I said in my most kingly manner as I raised my squirt gun and...

"In addition," Felinah, continued, "I would like to—"

And at this point, in an attempt to get Her Majesty to shut up and allow me to shoot Lord Andrés, I turned and squirted the Queen of Caid in the face with my squirt gun.

WARNING TO FUTURE MONARCHS: Do NOT squirt the Queen of Caid in the face with a squirt gun! Nobody thinks this is funny, and it is a disrespectful and completely inappropriate means of treatment of the First Lady of Grace and Beauty of the kingdom. These facts were explained to me by a group of concerned individuals—including Duchess Ceinwen, Baroness Emrys, Duke

The Reign At Pennsic Falls Mainly On The Plain or Postcards From The Throne, Part 3

Edric, and even the Baron and Baroness of Hidden Mountain—in a conversation which was surprisingly frank and sincere considering it was being conducted with the sovereign monarch of a recognized SCA kingdom who had to shout in order to be heard through the duct tape covering the port-a-potti door. I would probably still be in there today if Ceinwen had not realized that they neglected to remove the Crown from my head before taping the door shut.

◆ ◆ ◆

I'd love to tell you about the rest of the spectacle of Pennsic, but frankly, there just isn't room or time to do so. For seven days we had the honor of personifying Caid in the eyes of the Known World—fortunately, we had plenty of help in that job. Everyone who was there to support us, advise us and just stand beside us, did their part to show what a shining gem our kingdom truly is. We had a lot of wonderful moments as king and queen, but I'm not sure we were ever more proud to be Caidans than we were as we drove away from Pennsic, headed home, ready to begin the second half of our reign.

Fangs For The Memories: Medieval Halloween Monsters

When I was a child, one of my favorite pastimes was to read a good book. And by "good," I mean "gruesome, horrifying and filled with spooks and goblins." I spent many evenings reading novels with titles like, *The Bloodthirsty Thing That Lives In Your Attic*. Unfortunately, after wading through 75 pages of extraneous babble like character development, symbolism and expository dialogue, I'd finally come to the book's crucial, suspense-filled moment:

"…when Countess Abattoir noticed the draperies in the darkened upstairs study stirring before an unfelt gust of air. 'Strange,' thought she, 'no window nor flue should be open with a storm raging outside. This unwelcome breeze must have extinguished the candles I left burning upon the table.' Then, the Countess stepped into the shadowy room and pulled back the curtains to find—"

And this would be exactly the point at which my mother said, "It is time for bed, young man, and I am not going to tell you again!"

Which, of course, meant I had to continue reading under the covers with a flashlight that I'd stashed beside my bed "for emergencies." Typically, after reading stories of soul-stealing, flesh-rending, blood-drinking supernatural freaks until well after midnight (because I certainly wasn't going to be *sleeping* any time soon), the batteries in my flashlight would be exhausted and I would spend the next few hours huddling beneath the blankets listening to the sounds of demons converging around my bed. Finally, just as I began to think that perhaps the monsters had gotten bored and I had a chance of surviving the night, one of our cats would make the mistake of jumping onto my mattress looking for a warm place to sleep, which would send me fleeing into the living room to chase away the spooks by blockading the door with my mother's good china and setting the sofa on fire.

Similarly (although with slightly less hysteria), in the Middle Ages, the turning of the seasons made people contemplate the presence of monsters and malevolent spirits as the lengthening shadows of autumn crept a little closer to their doorsteps each evening. With Halloween lurking around the corner like a carnivorous ghoul, I thought this might be an appropriate time to examine this type of medieval folklore with as much meaningful research as possible in the brief period of time during which I am able to restrain myself from ripping open the six bags of candy Felinah just brought home from the grocery store.

Matters Of Grave Importance

As gypsy immigrants from the Asia Minor and India began to arrive in Eastern Europe in the 15th century, they brought with them ghastly tales of bodies rising from graveyards to prey upon the living. They called these undead creatures, *bhuta, mullo* or, the term we are most familiar with, *vampires*.

Medieval vampires weren't quite as sexy and glamorous as the their 21st century counterparts, however. While we think of vampires as suave and seductive and able to leap tall buildings in a single bound, the stories of medieval vampires portray them as pesky, smelly, unpredictable nuisances—sort of a cross between a crazy neighbor and a stray dog.

According to legend, there were a number of ways by which an individual could become a vampire. For example, if a cat jumped over a corpse before it was buried, it would become a vampire. It was also believed that the seventh child of the same gender born into a family would turn into a vampire after death. Additionally, anyone might become a vampire for no better reason than meeting their demise in an unusual fashion, including (according to various of stories from the period) being kicked by a horse, falling off a moving wagon, improper dental hygiene, tragic cheese-making accidents or choking on particularly stout ale.

In fact, medieval vampires didn't even have to be human. Some legends describe vampiric animals and even plants. According to one source, a squash or melon could become a vampire (no, I'm not kidding about this) if it was left on the counter too long. Vampire vegetation would "begin to move, make noise and show blood." Think about *that* next time you see some slimy cucumber you've forgotten about down in the bottom of your vegetable crisper.

Fortunately, getting rid of a medieval vampire was much easier than the elaborate, dramatic methods we see today in documentaries like *Buffy the Vampire Slayer*. One of the easiest and most common means to defeat a vampire was to scatter millet or poppy seeds around its grave. For some reason, people thought vampires had some kind of bizarre mathematical obsession, and would spend all night trying to count these tiny kernels of grain rather than drinking blood. (It does make you wonder if the choice of Dracula's title as "count" was purely coincidental.)

One Russian tale tells of a man who was riding by a graveyard when he saw a vampire climbing out of his tomb. (The vampire's tomb, that is, not the man's.) According to this story, the vampire was carrying the lid to his coffin, which he set down on the steps of the nearby church before going about his nightly vampire business. The man then took the coffin lid away, and the vampire was destroyed when the sun came up the next morning, because he couldn't return to his tomb without the coffin lid—sort of like trying to return from a business trip without the proper receipts and expense reports, I suppose.

The hawthorn tree was often used as a ward against vampires. In some places, a sprig of hawthorn was slipped into the stocking of a corpse during the funeral to prevent it from walking among the living again as a vampire. Apparently the theory was that vampires might have the power to cheat death, leave their graves, fly through the air and steal people's souls, but they certainly couldn't figure out how to remove an uncomfortable little stick from their shoe.

A Howling Good Time

Just about every little town or village in the Middle Ages seemed to have a legend about some crazed hermit, deranged old woman or antisocial psychopath who was rumored to transform into an animal and roam the countryside causing all sorts of mayhem and terror. Throughout Europe, there were stories of people changing into cats, foxes, bears, dogs, ferrets, wallabies, crickets, dandelions, skinks, "those little rolly bugs" and various other fearsome creatures and barnyard pests. These shape-changers were sometimes called *bisclavaret*, *garwal*, or *loup-garou*. Thanks to the cheesy horror pictures of the 1950s, however, we are probably most familiar with the one known as the *werewolf*.

There aren't a whole lot of good medieval explanations as to why someone would gain the ability to change into a wolf. By scientific analysis of contemporary eyewitness accounts, we can see that many of these individuals were, as we would say in modern, clinical terminology, "not playing with a full deck." These "werewolves" seem to be the kind of people who, today, would be discovered with body parts in their cellars and human heads in their refrigerators. When apprehended by the authorities, they simply resorted to: "I couldn't help it! I'm an animal! *Arf! Arf! Woooo...!*"

According to medieval folklore, the werewolf "lurks within the thick forest, mad and horrible to see," sort of like certain members of the chivalry on Sunday morning at a war when the merchants are out of coffee. One source says that, after taking on their animal shapes, werewolves would roam the countryside "living on prey and roots." I am sure you can see how a savage creature prowling through the darkness stalking innocent parsnips would strike terror into the hearts of villagers and townsfolk.

In the Middle Ages, you didn't need a silver bullet or a +4 magic sword to deal with a werewolf. The challenge was not in dispatching the murderous creature, but rather in discovering who was taking the form of this supernatural beast. Typically the culprit was found out when they revealed a "sympathetic wound" shortly after some brave soul went on a werewolf hunt. One story from France tells of a farmer who chased a werewolf with an axe and cut off one of its paws. He then spent several days trying to track this three-legged beast, but he didn't solve the mystery until he noticed that his wife hadn't moved from her seat by the hearth for quite some time. When he questioned her, he noticed that *one of her hands was missing*! (We can assume the farmer was probably not nominated for the town's "Mr. Observant" award.)

◆　　◆　　◆

Of course, if you don't feel like hunting through creepy forests or frequenting local graveyards in search of werewolves and vampires, don't forget the simplest means of dealing with such creatures: bribery. On Halloween night, people in the Middle Ages left nuts and treats at their doorsteps to appease the prowling monsters. Even today you'll find that a bowl of Snickers bars and Reese's peanut-butter cups beside the front door is a pretty good deterrent against any shape-shifting tree frogs or a bloodthirsty zucchinis which might be stalking your neighborhood on October 31. I'm planning on leaving a package of Three Musketeers by my door and curling up to relax with a good Stephen King novel.

The Romance of the Sword

Beginning at a very young and impressionable age, I wanted a sword. At the same time most of my friends were pestering their parents for motorcycles, electric guitars and fully automatic firearms, I incessantly asked my mother to buy me a sword and, in response, she told me that I was too young and irresponsible to have one.

I was immediately determined to prove her wrong. In order to do this I did just what any responsible person would—I got a saw, went to our tool shed and hacked three feet off the handle of an otherwise perfectly good shovel. This yard-long piece of tapered hardwood became my wooden "sword." (And yes, in answer to your question, I *did* put the shovel head with its remaining 18 inches of handle back in the tool rack—it just didn't occur to me that there was anything *wrong* with this.)

After several years of unrelenting nagging and whining, my parents finally agreed to buy me a sword as a reward for one of the few good things I did as a child. (I don't remember what it was.) Their only requirement was I had to tell them where to find it.

That was a real stumper. In all of my begging, I had never considered *where* to obtain a sword, I only knew that I *wanted* one. I told them to try some antique shops, but they never found any swords, and I didn't know where else to look. (And, in light of what happened when I finally *did* get a sword, I'm glad they didn't spend several hundred dollars to buy me a valuable antique—but I'm getting ahead of myself.)

The Role Of The Sword

As I grew up, my fascination with swords and medieval weaponry was inflamed by the discovery of fantasy role-playing games, which are responsible for introducing many otherwise well-adjusted teen-agers to the concept of spending all their spare time and discretionary income on truly meaningless hobbies.

In high school I met with a group of young men who played "swords and sorcery" games each day in the school library when they probably should have been doing their homework. Then, after a prolonged session of slaying dragons and battling evil wizards, we all piled into the two working automobiles we had, and on the trip home engaged in such valiant and heroic acts as leaping from car to car at 40 mph on a deserted country two-lane road, and jockeying for position so that all the guys in the lead car could spit on the windshield of the car behind.

The members of this cadre of troublemakers were always searching for ways to make or scavenge armor, weapons and other quasi-medieval accouterments. What we wound up with was innovative if not authentic, such as a cuirass made from an old jacket interwoven with bailing wire (and let me tell you, *that* was a comfy garment!), a dagger made from 14" bolt pounded (mostly) flat, and a spear made from a sharpened wooden rod we kidnapped from one of our closets without letting our parents know ("Hey, those clothes didn't *really* need to hang up.").

The best discovery of all, however, came one afternoon during a trip to the Army surplus store to buy kerosene lanterns for an expedition into an abandoned mine shaft nearby (remember, we lived in the country and we had an amazing lack of parental supervision). There, in a bin at the back of the store, was a bundle of rusty Army machetes marked $3.95 each. They weren't glorious weapons of King Arthur or Beowulf, but to us they were the next best things to a real sword. Each member of the group bought one.

As you might imagine, we were not content to merely *have* these crude sword-like weapons. We felt the need to *use* them. On each other.

Saturday Night Fights

One Saturday evening we had scheduled a role-playing game at a house belonging to the grandparents of one of our friends. His grandparents had gone on vacation for the summer and had left our friend *specific instructions* to keep the house safe and not to let anything get damaged.

As we were making extensive preparations for this game—such as procuring nearly lethal quantities of potato chips and Oreo cookies without our parents' permission—we were inspired by the idea of springing an ambush on our friends in true medieval adventurer tradition. With a quick foraging trip through a few of our kitchens we came up with the weapons for our ambush: eggs, tomatoes, oranges and, our most awesome weapon, a pump-pressurized fire extinguisher.

We filled the fire extinguisher with water, but that seemed to lack the authority we wanted, so we put in a little laundry soap for good measure. Then, we added some perfume. And some sour milk. Some window cleaner, lemon juice, mouthwash, maple syrup and finally some bug spray. At last we figured the noxious mixture was sufficiently disgusting that we could risk spraying our friends with it, so we pressurized the fire extinguisher and drove off.

Our plan was to creep up to the house (where, remember, no adults were in residence), launch a fusillade of eggs and tomatoes at the living room window, then, when everyone came running outside, to hose them down with the fire extinguisher. Unfortunately, we hadn't counted on them *expecting* this and planting someone on top of the nearby patio with a countermeasure—in the form of a 50-pound bag of Purina Dog Chow—to prevent our attack. The counter-ambusher sprang up, catching us in mid-creep, and began blasting everyone with handfuls of rock-hard Dog Chow nuggets as we all scattered for cover.

Fortunately, the fellow with the fire extinguisher saved us all by discharging the contents at our ambusher, who immediately dropped his Dog Chow and ran for the edge of the roof with both hands over his mouth. The poor fellow didn't even get that far before he became *violently* ill having been soaked with a mixture that I'm sure could have stripped paint from the hull of a battleship.

Then the rest of the crew came screaming out of the house, machetes drawn, hurling their own eggs, tomatoes and other garbage. A grand sword fight ensued—which, I want to stress, was totally safe because everyone had turned their machete blades around and was striking with the *unsharpened* edges. (Yeah, right.) During the course of the evening several windows were broken, Dog Chow was scattered in every room of the house, a small tree in the front yard was chopped down and one fellow wound up with the "dull" edge of a machete stuck into his hand.

No fatalities were reported, although there were rumors about what happened to our friend when his grandparents returned from their vacation. We never heard from him again.

The romance of the sword had infected us all, inspiring us with the desire for glory, honor and a certain level of craziness. A few years later, several members of the fantasy gaming group joined a club called the SCA hoping to recapture the fun and friendship of that wild, magical evening—as well as several others that I dare not recount in print.

Sometimes, on a lazy summer evening when the fighting is done and I'm relaxing in my pavilion enjoying the long twilight, I think back on those days when I was new to the Society. I was totally unaware of how the group worked, the personalities involved or the politics that went on behind the scenes. All I knew was, after many years of wishing, I had found a group of people who, like me, had rediscovered the romance of the sword—with the added benefit of not having to dodge flying Dog Chow in lists combat.

From time to time I raise my sword in salute of those friends long past and those yet to come, all of whom still yearn to recapture the glory.

Chronicles of the Inquisitor, Part 2

In this chapter, the mysterious chronicler known only as "The Inquisitor," an omniscient being who inexplicably lives in Guillaume's guest room closet, relates another story of the "behind the scenes" events that occurred during the reign of Guillaume and Felinah.

◆ ◆ ◆

At Pennsic War—the SCA's biggest gathering—a monarch has an obligation to set an example of service to the Society. At last year's war, when the event stewards were having trouble finding enough workers, they came to each of the kings at the event to ask them to "pitch in" by recruiting volunteers from the members of their populace.

When the volunteer autocrat approached Guillaume, he wasted no time in setting a valiant example by announcing in his most regal voice that he would personally serve on the midnight shift at the toll gate. Of course, this announcement would probably have been much more effective at inspiring his populace to action if he had made it on the battlefield or while judging the arts and sciences display, rather than while eating his sixth plate of pancakes at the all-you-can-eat breakfast bar in the food court, but his intentions were noble.

Luckily, a king cannot be unaccompanied, even while eating pancakes, and Guillaume's proclamation was overheard by a large entourage of peers and kingdom officers who immediately knew that they too would be obliged to work at the gate alongside their monarch.

So it was that Guillaume arrived at the Pennsic toll gate for the midnight shift accompanied by his queen, his official "handler," Duchess Ceinwen, the captain of his guard, Lord Hrodnavar, the Kingdom Exchequer, Mistress Asgerdr, his chamberlain, Lady Ceridwen, and Baroness Cara. If you think this rather impressive staff would be sufficient to keep the king from causing havoc, you vastly underestimate the ability of our former king to cause havoc.

Felinah and Ceinwen, fully aware of Guillaume's inability to deal with any task involving numbers, money, filing, organizing, spelling or accurately recording details in any fashion, found a position which was ideally suited to his talents: Pennsic gate greeter. They felt that people arriving at Pennsic would be delighted to be welcomed by a king! (Which would undoubtedly have been true if they were referring to a king who was dignified and regal, such as, say, the King of Calontir.)

Guillaume was soon joined in his war-greeting duties by Rowen and Crysigon, and the three of them, lacking any form of productive activity to keep themselves occupied, began critiquing the job performance of the Caidans who were actually trying to get some work done. Within moments they decided that the statements being made by the gate staff—"Have a great war!" "Enjoy your stay!" "Welcome to Pennsic!" etc.—constituted illegal endorsements of the event. From then on, Guillaume decreed that, in accordance with FCC regulations, the only sentiment that could be offered by the gate staff was the neutral, generic, non-judgmental phrase: "Have a Pennsic."

If this had been any random lunatic annoying the staff, the constables would have solved the problem by simply summoning the sheriffs and having him removed from the site. But this was the King of Caid who, you'll recall, came to the gate specifically to set an example of duty and service for the people of his realm, and who then spent the next several hours urging the gate crew to tell people weary from long plane-rides and cross-country car trips to, "Have a Pennsic!" These people undoubtedly thought the toll gate had been staffed by the local asylum—but, on the positive side, it did make the lines move faster.

Then, shortly after midnight, a car roughly the size of several New England Townships pulled up to the gate. Out of this exceptionally large automobile emerged an exceptionally large man who looked like he'd been in the automobile for an exceptionally long time. He was somewhere between 6'4" and 10' tall, and he resembled the Incredible Hulk, except that he was slightly bigger and less inclined toward polite conversation.

As the guy lumbered into the gate pavilion, Ceinwen cheerfully summoned him to the registration table hoping she could distract him before Guillaume, Crysigon and Rowen started giving him a hard time. She asked the standard list of check-in questions and it looked like the process might conclude without incident when she came to the last piece of required information: "What's the name of the household you'll be camping with?"

And he answered proudly: "Clan McGroin!"

The words echoed through the tent like a gunshot, and for a moment everyone was silent. Then the royal greeting posse decided that this was possibly the funniest household name in the history of the universe, and with all the tact and subtlety of a trio of nightclub hecklers, Guillaume and crew began asking, "Hey, is there an Amish fellow in your household named 'Grabb? Is your fastest runner named 'Flash'? Are members from the New World called, 'Yank'?" and so on.

At this point Duchess Ceinwen knew that unless she took immediate action the morning headline on the *Philadelphia Gazette* was going to read: "California Man's Body Found Floating In Monongahela River With Crown Stuffed In Mouth." She quickly told the fellow that he was the lucky winner of a free entrance to the war, and that he didn't have to fill out any more forms or wait in any more lines and that his admission would be personally paid by the King of Caid as soon as His Majesty returned from the restroom and scolded the court jester for wearing the Crown in his absence.

Fortunately, the large man seemed satisfied by this, so he stepped outside, picked up his car and walked off toward the Clan McGroin campsite.

This is a true and accurate account of the events that transpired upon the said day, as I witnessed them. May the angels have mercy upon the souls of all those involved, especially those who may be recognized upon the battlefield in the future by large, armed members of Clan McGroin.

By my hand,
The Inquisitor
To Be Continued...

School of Hard Knatts

College. The greenhouse wherein young minds sprout in the light of knowledge and stretch toward new ideas. This was the environment in which the computer programming students at my college made their way every morning to the Engineering Quad to further their mastery of technology by exchanging on-line pornography and discussing how to reach level 22 of "Star Empire Nemo-Galaxia," and where burly, tattooed men in faded blue jeans gathered at the Industrial Arts Building to learn how to spit and charge me $97.35 per hour to inform me that the particular model of fan belt used in my car is no longer being manufactured and must be shipped in from an automotive parts "collector" in upstate New York…

(He's completely raving now. Please pay no attention. We're sure he will get to the point of this chapter in just a moment.—*The Editor*)

Fortunately, as an English Literature major, I was spared the necessity of learning any skills that might be applied to a career in the real world. I did, however, spend a great deal of time learning about the Renaissance. During this portion of my education, I was introduced to the concept of the "Renaissance Man"—a person who is knowledgeable in the fields of science, philosophy, art and athletics.

In one particular essay—written by da Vinci or Moliére or Clousseau or some other immortal writer of the period whose name totally escapes me—we were given a list of the qualities of a Renaissance Man, one of which I remember very specifically: "He must play well at tennis and other games with the ladies."

Since I wanted to be a well-rounded Renaissance Man, I was excited when, at one of the first tournaments I ever attended—back when I thought fighting was a violent and brutal ritual I never wanted to participate in—the herald announced there would be games held on the lawn after the fighting was done.

When the lists were finished, Master Tryggvi met with a group of young SCA members—most of whom, like me, were too young to fight—and explained the rules to a game he called *Knattlikker* (or some silly Scandinavian spelling like that). For those of you who are unfamiliar with this game, allow me to recount the history Master Tryggvi taught us that day.

To Play Or Knatt To Play

The Vikings, it seems, lacked the particular technology required to master the difficult construction of a "ball." One day, however, young Olav Kürtennrod and his father Svvennsi Smorgasboardson were walking through the woods when a sharp, heavy hunk of wood broke loose from a tree branch high above. The knot plummeted toward earth where it struck Svvennsi in the head, killing him instantly.

"Hey, that vas pretty kül," said Olav (in Norwegian, obviously) as he picked up the wooden burl and wiped away the blood and brains. "Ve kould make a game out ov this!"

So Olav set out to create a sport utilizing an irregularly shaped hunk of hardwood as a projectile. He quickly discovered that with his bare hand he was unable to throw this knot of wood hard enough to obtain lethal velocities, so Olav devised a stick (or, in Norse, "stykke") that he could use to fling the knot with enough force and accuracy to kill, or at least maim his friends.

Olav also designed a playing field covered with broken glass and razor blades, and two goals pierced with long, rusty spikes and surrounded by a 10-foot zone of slippery whale blubber, but these game features never really caught on. Instead, the Norwegians played Knattlikker on a rectangular field with a four-foot goal post at either end.

Each team of 10 players would carry the knot with their sticks and attempt to strike the goal post with it. This could be accomplished either through a masterful strategy of moving players down the field utilizing a calculated balance of offensive and defensive tactics, or by using the knot to injure enough of the opponents that one man could walk to the other goal uncontested.

Knatt In My Back Yard

Master Tryggvi's re-creation of Knattlikker contained all the fun and excitement of the original Viking sport, with the added benefit of being only slightly less dangerous. Our SCA "knot" was an oblong hunk of duct-taped foam about the same weight, size and softness of an under-ripe cantaloupe. The sticks were racquetball racquets from which the original strings were removed and replaced with loosely woven macramé cord, creating more of a scoop than a paddle and increasing the chance of dislocating another player's finger should they have the poor judgment to place their hand too close to the stick.

School of Hard Knatts 67

The rules were simple and similar to SCA combat: If the knot hit a player's arm or leg, they lost that limb. If the knot struck a player's head or torso, the player was "dead" until the next point was scored. This created a very interesting competition which was unlike anything in modern sports except maybe professional hockey—after only a few seconds one team had a wide numeric advantage due to casualties (one of the most successful strategies to take control of the game was to kill the "center" with the knot as soon as it was put into play), and many of the surviving players were hopping around the field on one foot.

In order to prevent real injuries due to players' personal bodies colliding with sticks moving at high rates of speed, Tryggvi thoughtfully covered the edge of the racquets with garden hose. Unfortunately, this hose had all the protective resilience of reinforced concrete, as I learned in my first game of Knattlikker when, as I was diving for the knot, Lady Aurelia attempted to insert her stick into my nose in a successful effort to keep me from scoring. Ouch! (Or, in Norse, "Öuch!")

In those days nearly every Calafian baronial event concluded with a game of Knattlikker. Our teams had names like "Odin's Raiders," and "Battle Trolls," and we had no hesitation about playing for several hours, running the equivalent of six or seven hundred miles, only to be put out of the game permanently by a stick across the jaw. (Or worse—we weren't smart enough to wear groin protection during these games, you see.) For some reason—perhaps complaints by the local trauma unit—the game of Knattlikker faded away, but it has always been a fond memory of mine.

I am reminded of all this because, at the most recent baronial war, Master Tryggvi resurrected Knattlikker following closing court on Sunday. As one of the few surviving members of the barony who had actually participated in Knattlikker games as a youth (or, in Norse, "Jute"), Master Tryggvi called me out to the field to be one of the line judges.

I was amazed to see how young the players were. Most of them weren't even old enough to *fight* for cryin' out loud. They didn't quite get the overall perspective of the game at first—they seemed to be fixated on actually scoring points. Then one of the line judges called a player on a leg shot and little light bulbs flashed above their young heads all across the field. "Hey, we can use this thing *offensively!*" Before long they were out in the thick of the game, hobbling around with wounded limbs, littering the field with opponents' bodies, sacrificing themselves to defend their goal, and hurling the knot like the great Viking heroes of old.

We finally put a halt to the game about an hour later when everyone (line judges included) was exhausted and one of the young men took a stick across the face in a furious rush for the goal. (Öuch!) Final score: Deathbringers 5, Bloodletters 2.

There was something special about those games of Knattlikker in my early days in the Society. Maybe it was the camaraderie and competition of the game, maybe it was the excitement and physical exertion, or maybe it was just brain damage caused by repeated head blows, but Knattlikker kept bringing me back to the SCA, giving a clumsy, inartistic young man a chance to be a part of the Current Middle Ages.

I bet we'll be seeing more of the Knatlikker game at coming SCA events—or at least, I hope we will. If so, you can count on me to be there with my running shoes (and my groin protection) on. If you see us playing, come on out and give it a try. What have you got to lose (beside a few teeth)?

The Dramatic Lessons of History

When my book *This Sovereign Stage* was published recently, I was thrilled by the response among the SCA's academic community. Several of the most respected historical experts in the kingdom, including Mistress Maria-Theresa and my own mother, applauded my scholarly observations of theater in the Middle Ages with comments like: "Danny Kaye's *The Court Jester* is not a primary resource," and "*Hamlet* wasn't a Scandinavian breakfast sandwich," and "Don't you think you should have done some actual research before writing this book?"

Clearly, I realized, they had missed the point of my writings about the medieval theatrical tradition. My book wasn't about painstaking research and historical detail. It was based on one overarching premise that served as both a philosophical thesis and an analytical presupposition, thereby creating *de facto donnée* for my belles-lettres, which was this: Medieval theater was really bad.

Thus, in order to dispel any rumors that my research into thespian history was either faulty or, God forbid, fabricated, in this chapter I would like to present an overview of theater and drama from antiquity to the Middle Ages. Then, when I get finished, I'm going to go eat my Hamlet and bacon.

Classics on the Boards

Experts have a hard time agreeing on when the art form we know as theater began. (That's primarily due to the fact that "experts" tend to be a bunch of self-important blowhards who would probably have a hard time agreeing on what kind of pizza to order for lunch.) Most believe that the origins of drama are lost in the mists of time, probably around 30,000 years ago when one Neolithic caveman accidentally hit another with a mastodon bone and a crowd of onlookers laughed themselves silly.

One of the earliest documented theatrical presentations began in Egypt around 2500 B.C. when priests created the *Memphite Drama*. This multi-part ritualistic show, performed on the first day of spring, was a re-enactment of the murder of the god Osiris by his brother Seth. (Thus creating a form of theatrical interaction that can be seen today on *The Jerry Springer Show*.) The Memphite

Drama was staged annually for more than 1,900 years—a record for continual performance that was only recently surpassed by the Broadway run of *Oh! Calcutta!*

Theater as we know it, however, began in Greece in the 6th century B.C. There, presentations of tragic drama were performed as part of the *City Dionysia*, a festival whose name is derived from the fact that naming a festival after a mythological god sounds much more sophisticated than calling it, "six days of drunken riots."

Although early stage productions focused on themes of death, betrayal, horror, sacrifice and grief, the Greeks soon invented the concept of "comedy" when audiences, having sat through several hundred hours of suicides, incest, betrayals and anguish, realized that they needed to (as theatrical scholars say) "lighten up."

The greatest of all Greek comedy writers was Aristophanes, whose works include *The Clouds*, *The Wasps*, *The Frogs*, *The Dingoes*, *The Police*, *The Rolling Stones*, and that cult classic, *The Thesmophoriazusae*. But undoubtedly the greatest of all Aristophanes' work is *The Birds*, which includes such brilliant comic scenes as the two main characters being startled by a slave jumping out of a thicket and, in response, defecating on stage. (As God is my witness, I'm not making that up!)

Roman Around the Theater

Greek theater came to an end in 404 B.C. when the Spartans invaded Athens after learning that matinee tickets for *Miss Saigon* were sold out. After this, theatrical performance moved to Rome where it took on a very different aspect.

In Rome, dramatic productions were staged as part of the Imperial festivals, which took place approximately every 48 minutes. This was good in the sense that there was lots of theater in Rome, but it was bad in the sense that stage plays had to compete with other forms of entertainment, such as gladiators, chariots, prisoners being fed to wild animals, exotic dancers, NAASCAR races, and Britney Spears concerts. And lets face it, when you have a choice between watching people in masks mince around a stage for three hours or seeing someone get eaten by a bear…well, let's just say there's a reason that PBS has to beg for donations while guys with names like A-Train and Ultimo Dragon get paid millions of dollars to appear on the *WWF Smackdown*.

The most popular type of Roman theater, however, was called *mime*—a form of comedy that, as we would say today, was "intended for mature audiences only." In mime performances, viewers laughed at such delightful, humorous presentations as simulated sex on stage, obese people eating massive quantities of food, fist fights, actual sex on stage and public executions. Mime performances also included jugglers, acrobats, tightrope walkers, dancers and clowns—just to make sure the audience didn't get bored if there was a slow spot in the sex and violence.

In Roman theater, however, nothing could compare with the most popular target for comedic ridicule: Christianity. Many mime performances featured distorted parodies of baptism and mass, which is undoubtedly why playwrights and actors suddenly began to find themselves out of work when Christian emperors rose to power in the 2nd and 3rd centuries A.D. At the Trullan Council of 692, when Pope Sergius placed a ban on all forms of theatrical performance, His Holiness is said to have proclaimed, "Let's see thou laughest at excommunication, vile stage monkeys!"

The Theater Goes Dark (Age)

Drama took a brief hiatus for 300 years or so, but by the 10th century, theatrical performance began to appear again in (of all places) the church. These performances, which were put on as part of the services of the liturgical hours, were dignified and stylized to such a degree that many of the performers could have slipped into a coma and the audience would not have noticed for several days.

By the 12th century, however, the church began to authorize performance of Biblical plays for the general public, which were called *vernacular dramas*. These plays were sponsored and organized by trade guilds and professional associations. Guild members took time off of work to perform in dramas that ranged in subject matter from the martyrdom of various saints to…the martyrdom of various *other* saints. These plays, which had casts of several hundred amateur actors and required as many as 25 days to perform, were called *miracle plays*, as in, "If we ever get through this performance, it'll be a miracle!"

Another popular type of medieval drama was the *morality play*, in which actors personified various allegorical concepts in an attempt to show the perils of sinful behavior. Morality plays, like the famous *Castle of Perseverance*, went on for hours and hours and *hours*, during which actors playing roles like "chastity," "industry" "shrift" and "abstinence" tried to convince the audience to spurn other characters like "lechery," "gossip," "lust," and "profit." In a demonstration of just how effective this was, the church banned the performance of morality plays in the 15th century because the "sin" characters had become far more popular with viewers than the "virtue" characters—another example of the huge entertainment potential of good role models.

Church reform in the 16th century brought an effective end to the religious-themed plays of the Middle Ages, but opened the door for a revival of professional, popular theater. Actors and authors began experimenting with subjects as diverse as classical mythology, national history and romantic comedy. Soon, writers like Kyd, Marlowe, Jonson and Shakespeare were seeking to explore, not divine majesty nor miraculous occurrences, but realistic human emotions and actual historical events through that most powerful of all the playwright's tools: special effects.

◆ ◆ ◆

From the dawn of time to the present day, theater has played a very unique role in human culture—allowing us to better understand the nature of reality through the presentation of imaginary characters, places and events. Like all art forms, theater reflects political, social and cultural trends, yet it is singularly unique: Unlike sculpture, painting or literature, the art of theater is insubstantial. It exists only for a moment, then disappears, and can never be re-created in exactly the same manner.

Theater is both very primitive and very complex, reaching into the dark yearnings of our past, and reflecting our brightest hopes for the future. When the lights go down and the curtain rises, we, like audiences from Greece, Rome and medieval Europe, can see that "all the world's a stage" and we can be proud and amazed at the parts we all play in the drama of life, even if we do still laugh ourselves silly when someone gets hit with a mastodon bone.

Reigny Days and Mondays
or
Postcards From The Throne, Part 4

When you wear the Crown, your smile becomes the smile of the kingdom, and you feel an obligation to always put on the best face you can for your subjects. Few people see what goes on behind the thrones; fewer still appreciate the uncanny ability that the Crown itself has to change someone's life, to bring things into focus that were previously unclear. That ability comes at a price, however, and that price is time. There is little time to appreciate the special moments that you are privileged to enjoy. Savor them before they slip past forever…

♦ ♦ ♦

It is June and we're back at Coronation in the Barony of Dreiburgen. It's approximately 175 degrees inside the pavilion erected as a staging area to contain the gargantuan production that our stepping-up has become. Inside the tent are dozens of sweaty guys in full mail waiting to escort the new king to his throne, a harem of women in various stages of dress surrounding the soon-to-be-queen, a flock of proto-courtiers and guards who're not quite sure what their jobs are just yet, and a steady parade of kingdom officials who've come to gently check up on the couple who will inherit the mantle of state within the hour—all waiting for word that the final court of Edric and Battista has come to a close.

In the corner is an older fellow—notable in his Norman tunic, cowboy boots and Levi jeans—quietly holding a video camera and smiling a smile that conveys some combination of patience, amusement and enlightenment. Everyone else has seen the ritual of the passing of the Crown dozens of times; for him, this is a new experience.

My father has never quite understood the SCA. He's tolerated it, and he's even been to a few events just to see what this group his nutty son is involved with is all about. I'm sure there have been many times he wished he'd had a normal child—someone he could brag about to his friends; someone he could talk Bowl Games with after Thanksgiving dinner; someone who would come to him for advice on power tools. Instead, he got a kid who can recite Shakespeare and is frequently seen wearing a garment that looks suspiciously like a dress.

But my dad knew enough about the SCA to understand that the concept of "winning Crown Tournament" was a pretty big deal. So, regardless of the heat, the chaos and the men in metal dresses, he resolved that if his son was going to become King, then, darn it, he was going to make the journey from his home in Idaho to be there to witness it—video camera in hand.

I don't know exactly what my father expected this day to be, but I'm pretty sure this wasn't it. The buzz of activity, the charge of emotion, the solemnity of ceremony, and acclaim of the populace…by the end of the day, when court, presentations and the feast are done and the people raise their goblets to toast the king and queen, my dad's eyes have that sort of spinning, dizzy look of a father who, for the sake of his son, has taken one too many turns on the Tilt-A-Whirl. Maybe that's the result of looking through the lens of the video camera while recording about six hours of footage. Or, maybe it's because he's surprised at what's become of his column-writing, dress-wearing, nut-case of a son.

◆   ◆   ◆

It is July and we're at the Festival of the Rose—the day upon which, according to ancient and revered tradition, the kingdom honors the queen with displays of the arts and sciences, and Count Joseph of Silveroak attempts to get the king in trouble by trying to convince him to blow off court and slip away for pizza and a movie.

I have valiantly resisted Joseph's pepperoni-scented siren song, however, and chosen to fulfill my royal obligation by attending court. Of course, I'll be the first to admit that court is much more enjoyable when you're in the Big Chair. You get the best seat in the house, you get snacks in between each item of business, and if you're good, people even bring you presents. They bow before you and defer to you and generally make you feel like—well, like the king. Like the supreme and honored patriarch of the clan.

Now, the herald announces another presentation with a rather cryptic introduction: "Your Majesties, a traveling gypsy seeks an audience with you." We tell the herald to call forward this nameless petitioner. Imagine my surprise when up steps my father—Norman tunic, cowboy boots, blue jeans and all.

I'm not sure exactly what I was expecting from the Festival of the Rose, but I'm pretty sure this wasn't it—the sight of my own father, kneeling at my throne, calling me "Your Majesty." I'm already wondering how I'm going to explain this to my psychologist.

But my dad hasn't come to the Festival of the Rose just to help my psychologist put his children through college. He has come to make a donation—a rather *sizable* donation—to the kingdom travel fund. Of course, he didn't need to do it in this manner. He could have just given us an airline ticket voucher, or at the very least he could have handed a check to the exchequer. Instead, he contacted several of the people he'd met at Coronation, found out exactly how to go about making a formal presentation at court, and returned to Caid to participate in the group that made a king out of his nut-case son. It's quite a statement; quite a compliment.

And if my dad looked just a little thin and frail, or needed a little help getting back on his feet afterwards, well, I didn't notice. I was too busy being surprised.

◆ ◆ ◆

It is August and we've just returned home from Pennsic. It has been a long, exhausting trip and we are ready for an extended sabbatical during which we can recuperate, unpack in an orderly fashion, and contemplate the experiences of the past week. What we *have*, however, is four days to dump out the contents of our bags, wash the Pennsic-trademark nuclear orange mud out of every item of clothing, garb and regalia in our possession, and frantically re-pack for our trip to Western Seas, the Caidan barony in Hawaii. Not to mention catching up on the phone calls, e-mails and letters that have been accumulating in the absence of the king and queen. It's not likely to be a calm week.

And one of the things waiting for us is a phone message from my father: "Hope you guys had a great trip and a lot of fun. We can't wait to see all your pictures. Give me a call, okay? Oh, by the way, I'm in the hospital. Okay, talk to you soon."

Typical. So, needless to say, we put aside our whirlwind of royal activities for a few minutes to call and find out what's going on. When we finally get through to his hospital room, his wife answers. Dad is too weak to pick up the phone. It seems he collapsed a few days ago; when he was rushed to the hospital, the doctor found some "irregularities" in his pancreas. But don't worry, my step-mom says, it's just an ulcer. He'll be back on his feet in no time. No need to change any plans.

If her voice was a little tentative when she was giving us these reassurances, I didn't notice. I was a little too busy being...well, being king. I gave them our best wishes, hung up the phone and plunged back into the relentless business of the Crown.

◆   ◆   ◆

It is October and we are at Gyldenholt Harvest Tournament. Actually, I am, technically, *not* at Gyldenholt Harvest Tournament, although I am supposed to be. Instead, I am at my father's house in Idaho, keeping him company as he waits for the arrival of the home-care nurse whose job it will be to keep him comfortable for the next few days. After that, he won't need her services any more. That's all the time he has left.

The "ulcer" was a merciful fabrication, a lie of love. It's cancer. My dad insisted that we not be told the truth because he did not want Felinah and I to feel obliged to cancel our visit to Western Seas. He knew how important the trip was, how much work we'd put into being good monarchs, and he did not want us to neglect important Caidan business on his behalf. It was a sacrifice he was willing to make for the Crown.

And so, when we returned, we learned the truth. His cancer hadn't manifested itself until the final stages. By the time he'd begun to feel its effects, there was nothing the doctors could do but "keep him comfortable."

My father and I are also awaiting the arrival of Felinah, who stayed in Caid to take care of royal business at the tournament, then went straight from opening court to the Orange County airport to make the afternoon flight. Actually, the real reason she insisted on doing this was because my count's scroll, which will be presented to me in a few weeks at our stepping down, had its "unveiling" at Harvest Tourney. Felinah wanted to be there to take a photograph of the scroll to bring to my father—he was the one who commissioned it. This picture will be all he'll see of the spectacular piece of art made to commemorate his son's service as King of Caid. He won't be with us by the time Coronation comes 'round again.

But I don't know anything about this scroll as my dad and I sit together with the knowledge of his condition stifling our conversation. I only know that this is likely to be the last time we will have together, and I try not to let myself be distracted by kingdom business and royal issues as we sit quietly, patiently waiting. I'm not entirely successful.

Reigny Days and Mondays or Postcards From The Throne, Part 4

Finally, my dad asks to see the videotape of coronation again. We watch it together once more—the procession, the oath, the crowd cheering "Long live the king!" When it's done, my dad turns to me and says, simply, "I'm very proud of you, son." I don't know that I've ever heard that before. Or, maybe I have, but I was just too busy to notice. Maybe it took the weight of the Crown to make me hear.

◆ ◆ ◆

When you wear the Crown, your smile becomes the smile of the kingdom. Few people see what goes on behind the thrones; fewer still appreciate the uncanny ability that the Crown has to change someone's life. That ability comes at a price, however, and that price is time. There is little time to appreciate the special moments that come your way. Savor them before they slip past forever.

Knightly Attributes

What makes a knight? What are the defining qualities that a fighter must possess to be considered for the Order of Chivalry? Is there more to wearing a belt and spurs than just fighting? And, perhaps most importantly, can an entire chapter consist of nothing more than meaningless, rhetorical statements?

Unfortunately, the answer to the last of these questions is, "no," so we must look deeper into the concept of knighthood to understand the many aspects of this order, both in history and in the SCA. As my regular readers know, such understanding is obtained only through the kind of diligent and insightful research that can be conducted in the time it takes the delivery guy to get here with two orders of Spicy Yu Hsaing Shrimp and Krispy Egg Rolls that we have just ordered from *Wong's House of Mandarin Cuisine and Donuts*.

The concept of knighthood was brought to Europe by the Germanic tribes that swarmed over the crumbling Roman empire with all the grace and dignity of a busload of senior citizens shopping at a *Big Lots* "2 Fer A Buck" sale. Among these tribes, a young man was recognized as an adult after he underwent a "rite of passage" where the "tribal elders" bestowed the "accolade" by giving him a "slug in the mouth" and telling him to "get out." Thus was born the concept of the "knight errant," an angry, heavily armed young man wandering aimlessly around the countryside. As you might guess, this was a recipe for disaster.

Fortunately, someone at the beginning of the Middle Ages had the foresight to come up with the "code of chivalry" which dictated that, apart from whacking people with their swords, knights also had to be nice. *Un*fortunately, the earliest versions of the code of chivalry stated that knights pretty much only had to be nice to the king and the Pope, and even the king was somewhat questionable, so the rest of the population of Europe went on hiding in the forests for several centuries.

As the Middle Ages progressed, however, knights became more cultured, refined and genteel as education and civic contribution grew in importance. By the end of the Middle Ages, a knight was expected to be a scholar, an artist, a poet and a philosopher. The result of this cultural reform was that, by the late 16th century, the entire elite military class of Europe could have been defeated in combat by the Vienna Boys Choir. By the beginning of the Renaissance, many knights were deliberately and without provocation dressing in tights and wearing wigs, which was a certainly significant factor in the decline of chivalry in the Western world.

Knights In The SCA

Astute readers may recall the original topic of this chapter, which I believe was: "What does it take to be a knight?" As in the Middle Ages, a knight in the SCA must be skilled on the field, but there is more to it than that. A knight must also be thrifty, brave, loyal, trustworthy…no, wait. That's an Eagle Scout. A knight in the SCA must conform to a rigid and formal checklist of attributes that is considered by a large portion of the council of chivalry (by which I mean "me") when discussing a candidate for elevation to the order. Here are the universal and undisputed qualifications for knighthood from the "code of chivalry" transcribed in exacting detail from some obscure reference book I sort of remember reading at a party about 10 years ago:

• "A knight should be able to identify basic heraldic charges and blazon his own coat of arms." (Hint for fighters: "Blazon" has nothing to do with setting something on fire.)

Knowledge of heraldry is vitally important on the battlefield so that a knight can identify allies and enemies during the heat of combat when everyone is rendered anonymous by their armor. You can easily demonstrate this by asking any fighter what kind of armor some other fighter wears, to which the fighter will reply: "Oh, he has that stainless steel Corinthian helm with the black eagle wings on the sides and the breast plate that comes up over his shoulders like this and…" Then you can ask what the other fighter's heraldic device looks like and they will reply: "Ummmm…"

•"A knight should dance well and should know at least one court dance and one country dance."

You will probably not be surprised to learn that knights are masters of many medieval dances. After all, knights regularly display the ultimate in grace and poise on the battlefield—such as the time I broke my pole arm over Felinah's head while I was falling down an embankment during a bridge battle at kingdom war practice. When a knight steps out onto the dance floor at a revel, it is not uncommon for the other dancers to step aside and let the knight "have the floor" like John Travolta in *Saturday Night Fever*—especially if the knight has neglected to remove his sword, boots, spurs and belt, which are capable of inflicting bruises and lacerations on other dancers' shins at a distance of up 50 feet during a particularly energetic braisle. (For fighters who are not familiar with the terms, a "court dance" involves elegant steps that accentuate the grace of the dancers. A "country dance" involves sheep.)

- "A knight must sing and recite poetry with ease."

No doubt this will bring to mind the many times you have heard the knights of this kingdom performing period songs and ballads, such as Conté Cristian's popular rendition of the climactic aria from the famous medieval Spanish operetta, *Yo No Puedo Obtener No Satisfaçion*. Just as a knight must win battles with his skillful use of the sword and spear, so does a knight use romantic language and vivid description to become a master of verse and rhyme in order to, uh, talk really good at court and stuff.

- "A knight should play chess."

Chess teaches a knight many things: patience, strategy, forethought, determination and the desire to heave the chess board out of the revel hall and onto the nearby freeway when your opponent captures your queen and both rooks in exchange for a pawn and a drunken bishop. In addition, a knight should be familiar with some of the period versions of chess, like shatranj, which supplements the familiar game with such unique pieces as the camel, the catapult, the battering ram, the chariot, the giant flying insect, the space shuttle and the wealthy industrial tycoon.

- "A **knight** should deal chivalrously and courteously with persons of all stations at **all times**."

Let's **be honest** here: There is no single, defining checklist of activities that a fighter **must** fulfill in order to become a knight. Although many knights (and other **members** of the SCA) have their own expectations, the general goal is clear: to encourage everyone to contribute to the Society, and to show there is more to do in the SCA than hit your friends on the head with a stick.

Everyone has a personal list of the defining qualities that "make a knight," but paramount among them is the mature, responsible and courteous attitude we call "chivalry"—an outward and visible display of an inward and personal grace. That is the inextinguishable light that guides a knight along the path beyond the fighting field, through the dangers and hazards of the dance floor, the chess board, the herald's office and the bardic circle, transforming an angry, heavily armed adolescent into a gentle person who you seek out when you want enlightened, courteous conversation, or just want to get hit in the head with a stick.

Chronicles of the Inquisitor, Part 3

In this chapter, we read the final chronicle penned by the mysterious, shadowy figure called "The Inquisitor," who lives in Guillaume's guest room closet and emerges only when matters of great import need to be immortalized in writing or when there's a fresh pot of coffee brewing.

◆   ◆   ◆

For the people of Caid, October's Great Western War is the "final SCA gathering of the year," because that's much more poetic than saying, "one last bash with your buddies in armor." Everyone gets together to honor the glory of ages past, to accomplish feats of chivalry and valor, and to swill intoxicating drinks in fruit-shaped cups while howling at the moon.

Or at least, those seemed to be the goals that were set out at one recent GWW, and with the first two being completed successfully during daylight hours, everyone in camp began to pursue the third objective as soon as the sun went down.

King Guillaume and Queen Felinah first became aware of these activities when, after one of their typical evenings of wild debauchery and carousal, they returned to the royal pavilion at 8:22 p.m. and began to get ready for bed. Their preparations were quickly interrupted, however, by a sound that combined the tranquility of a shipwreck with the melodious tones of an industrial automobile crusher. Peeking out of the tent, Guillaume discovered that in the neighboring royal encampment, King Thorfinn of the West and his minister of trouble-making, Countess Berangaria de Montfort, had created something called a "margarita whacker" by combining a gas-powered Weed Eater mowing device with a Kitchenaid blender. Thus, every minute or so the authentic medieval atmosphere of the Western encampment was punctuated by a sound that went, and I quote, "rrr-RRRR-garrph-plu-plu-plu-morrROARRRR!!!" and could be detected on seismographs as far away as the Principality of Oertha.

In a stunning display of inter-kingdom diplomacy, Countess Berangaria had chosen to locate this mechanical abomination approximately 16" from the Caidan royal pavilion. After the second or third time the royal margarita whacker was powered up, Guillaume and Felinah realized they would not be getting to sleep any time before dawn, and so they put their Crowns back on their heads and ventured out again to see if they could find someplace more calm and relaxing, such as a prison riot.

Since they couldn't find a place that sedate, however, Guillaume and Felinah settled for the Hawaiian luau hosted by La Famiglia. This revel was noteworthy in the sense that there were, technically, no Hawaiians present, but it was the home of Caid's answer to the Western margarita whacker: The Iron Bartender competition. The rule of this competition was that various peers of the realm, who were hiding in the shadows behind the bar and praying that their king would not recognize them, had to mix "mystery drinks" with the ingredients provided by the judges, which seemed to be primarily: tequila, orange juice, seltzer, tequila, Gatorade, tequila and Drano.

While this competition was proceeding, the hosts of the party were doing their best to get everyone into the "spirit" by distributing authentic Hawaiian clothing which you are probably familiar with if you have seen documentaries on Polynesian life such as *Gilligan's Island*. Most of the Ladies of the Rose were wearing skimpy grass skirts, and needless to say, Guillaume did not want to be left out of this aspect of the Hawaiian luau activities, so, with the help of Lord Bart and Mistress Maria-Theresa, he selected a tasteful coconut-husk brassiere to wear along with his Crown and royal cloak.

(Fortunately, Countess Leonora was not on-hand to see this because she was working the late-shift at the gate. When Guillaume donned the coconut bra, however, the attendees of the luau rushed out of camp to summon a passing constable and asked him to radio the gate staff in order to find out if any visible smoke could be seen coming out of Leonora's ears as she detected this monumental disturbance in the Royal Force.)

The party went on for several hours and the guests had a marvelous time, excepting possibly the moment where Duke John caught on fire. When the cheesy Don Ho music had run out and the Iron Bartenders had used up all of their tequila and Gatorade, Guillaume and Felinah decided it was time to retire to their pavilion for the evening, but—and this is the important part—*Guillaume forgot that he was still wearing the coconut bra.*

A few minutes later, as Guillaume and Felinah were walking toward home, Duke Mathias of Atenveldt, one of the primary autocrats of the upcoming

Estrella War, approached them. Mathias greeted the king and queen with utmost respect, regardless of the fact that he had spent much of his evening at the margarita whacker, and said he had a Very Important Issue to discuss with them about the war.

Guillaume thanked his friend for his willingness to offer counsel to the monarch of an opposing kingdom, and bade Mathias to explain his concerns on the spot. Mathias said, "Your Majesty there are some details which you need to know as you prepare your policies for the negotiations which will affect the…"

And at this point Mathias' eyes traveled slowly downward toward Guillaume's chest, and suddenly the Very Important Issue was put on the back-burner as Mathias' mind struggled to review every item of reference material and historical documentation he'd ever read in order to see if a domed, symmetrical wooden chest protector was actually part of 15th century Burgundian fashion—or if it could possibly, maybe, conceivably be that the King of Caid was walking through camp dressed like a Hawaiian drag queen.

Then, remembering his station as a royal peer, Mathias assumed that the coconut bra was a delusion brought on by the margarita whacker, so he returned his gaze to Guillaume's face and continued: "S-s-so, what I mean is, in order to negotiate effectively, you need to know that…"

Then, certain that he had been hallucinating before, Mathias glanced down at Guillaume's chest, but when he saw that his eyes had not been playing tricks on him all thoughts of Estrella War were banished from his mind momentarily. Then, through sheer force of will, Mathias met Guillaume's eyes once again, but a moment later, as their conversation continued, his vision was drawn to Guillaume's chest once again—and this cycle continued repeatedly throughout their 30-minute discussion of the Very Important Issues facing Caid.

The result of this meeting was twofold: On one hand, Guillaume learned what it's like to try to conduct any sort of meaningful conversation if you're Anna Nicole Smith. On the other hand, one of the premier royal peers of Atenveldt discovered that the great and mighty army of Caid was being led by a King who dressed like Carmen Miranda.

This is a true and accurate account of the events that transpired upon the said day, as I witnessed them. Whether or not these events have anything to do with the fact that Caid and Atenveldt continue to engage in interkingdom war every spring over some sort of irresolvable differences, I cannot in truth say.

By my hand,
The Inquisitor
finis

Just Another Knight On the Wall

Traveling to a tournament in another barony is very enjoyable. It gives me the chance to enter the lists with a group of fighters I don't often meet in battle. It allows me to be pummeled into insensibility by some hulking duke who shapes his rattan swords by chewing on them with his teeth, or a glory-hungry young knight who trains with a radar gun and whose snaps have been clocked at over 300 mph. The mistress of the lists, in her infinite kindness, places me against such opponents in the first two rounds, ensuring that I will be knocked out of the competition by about 10:48 a.m. Then, I can enjoy watching the other fighters walk by my pavilion, shouting such words of comfort and encouragement as, "Hey Guillaume! Out in two, eh? Haw, haw!" and throwing marshmallows at me as they pass.

So it was that, at a recent tournament, having been eliminated from the competition, I met a fellow who came out to join me on the challenge field where the fighters who've been knocked out of the *real* competition gather to console themselves by beating one another senseless. The lord told me his name—Latke of Hamstring, or something like that—and said with great pride that this was his *very first event* in armor. He just walked right up and asked me if I would like to fight—apparently he didn't realize he was supposed to shrink with revered awe at the sight of my white belt.

The fellow's new armor sort of hung around him with all the panache of a 30 gallon trash barrel, and as he walked various pieces kept getting caught on one another; he had to do a little jig every two or three steps to get everything back into place. He'd borrowed someone's helm, which was too big, so he stuffed an old kneepad into the top to make it fit. Unfortunately the pad had slipped down over one eye, so he had to hold his head at a 45-degree angle to see.

As we began to fight, I realized that his ill-fitting vambraces prevented him from extending his arm, so to throw a blow he had to tilt his whole shoulder forward while simultaneously leaping sideways, and he looked kind of like a fiddler crab performing some sort of drug-induced mating dance. I let him hit my shield until he looked like he was about to pass out from exhaustion and the kneepad had nearly obscured his vision entirely, then I reached out with my sword and whacked him upside the helm.

With that, he made a noise which went, and I quote: "Ugguf," and spun around to his left as if he thought he might have been hit by someone who snuck up behind him.

"Did you do that?" he asked, trying to wiggle the kneepad out of his eye slot.

"Yes," I said, "and you might want to say *good* or you'll get hit again."

"Uhh, good. Wow. That was, like…good," he said, clearly waiting for me to explain what I had done and perhaps give him some pointers on how to keep it from happening next time.

I started to tell him about the importance of balance and the subtleties of sword orientation, but I had hardly said 10 words when his eyes began to glaze as he tried to absorb complex techniques that were far beyond his level of skill. So, with the sun beating down on my helm, I drew in a deep breath, stepped a little closer, and in a tone which implied that I was revealing a profound universal truth, said: "Look, just hit 'em with your sword, and block with your shield when you need to."

I'm not saying I'm proud of it, but *he* was delighted to think he was getting a knight's inside secrets, and *I* got to go sit in the shade. Everyone was happy.

Up Against The Wall

A few weeks later, my wife, Felinah, and I took a short vacation to visit her family in Mt. Shasta, a small town on the Oregon border that is known for a variety of wilderness activities and "extreme" outdoor sports. While there, we spent some time with Felinah's father, a tough ol' guy who organized the town's search-and-rescue team after returning from service in World War II.

During our visit Felinah's dad took us to the town's newly constructed outdoor activity center where, among other high-risk forms of entertainment, they've constructed a 30-foot artificial cliff where anyone can go to learn the treacherous art of rock climbing from highly trained instructors who look like they may have gotten their driver's licenses as long ago as last month.

As we were standing there, Felinah's dad said that watching those climbers reminded him of the time he rescued a lost hiker off a 2,000-foot vertical glacier during a blizzard with nothing but a toothpick and a ball of string while simultaneously fending off attacks by Nazi dive bombers with his hunting knife. Then, he softly cleared his throat—and to everyone else standing around it was just a throat clearing, but to me it was an unmistakable and concise statement that said:

"Fifty years ago I'd have mastered that puny little wall before breakfast, and I sure would like to tell my old friends down at the VFW hall that the man who married *my* little girl wasn't scared away by some silly toy rock. In fact, I bet you could climb right up that thing without breaking a sweat if you hadn't gone *out in two, pal!!!* Haw, haw!"

Suddenly, my mission was clear. A few minutes later, with a harness around my waist and rubber ballet slippers on my feet, I stepped up to the belayer (a nautical term meaning, "the person who holds the rope which keeps you from plunging to your bloody death") and asked for a turn on the wall.

The belayer was a nice lady whose arms were as graceful and delicate as the average forklift, and who was clearly an extremely skilled climber. She pointed to some particular spots on the wall that she claimed could be used as gripping points, and said some things about "grips" and "quirks" and "gnarls," but I didn't pick much of it up. I just hoped she wouldn't laugh too hard if I fell.

I climbed about 12 feet or so pretty easily, but then the going became a bit more difficult. I reached up for a couple of rock features, but I couldn't get a grip on any of them. Finally, after watching me fumble around for what seemed to be several weeks, the belayer said, "Put your left foot on that mogul by your knee, then reach up and catch that forky dingbat."

(I'm not sure if she actually said *forky dingbat* or not, but she kept using bizarre terms which seemed to have very specific meanings to her, but to me sounded like the names of bands on MTV.)

I found a little bump that was just big enough to hold with two fingers, and I managed to pull myself up. I thought it was a pretty spectacular move, but the belayer gave me a look which was somewhere between boredom and disdain and told me to pull my butt in.

I kept creeping upward until I was just about five feet from the top. At this point I made the mistake of glancing back at the ground and I realized that 25 feet is, in technical terms, a long way up. This did not make things any easier, and it was coupled with the fact that I couldn't seem to find anything to hold onto in order to climb the last few feet.

"Are you stuck?" the belayer asked.

"Um…yeah, I think."

"Here's a real power move you can do," she said. "Bring your foot up to that ledge on your right and haul yourself up the rest of the way."

I looked around for a moment. "You mean this ledge up by my *ear?*"

She rolled her eyes with a level of subtlety and discretion only a 17-year-old could muster, and said, "Okay then, reach up and catch that last hold straight above you."

I looked up and saw the "hold" she was talking about—a tiny protrusion about the size and shape of a light switch in the *off* position.

"I'm supposed to hold onto that?" I asked.

She snorted, "Wull…yuh!"

I reached up, hooked my finger onto this miniscule bump and tried to pull myself up. Unfortunately, I was largely unsuccessful in supporting my entire body weight with one finger, and I slipped off and plummeted three stories down to crash on the rocky ground below! Well, actually, because I was strapped into the harness and held up by my belayer, I swung down about four inches and then bonked against the wall like a goofus—but my stomach seemed pretty certain that it and I were going all the way to the ground as I was losing my grip on the forky dingbat.

"Yeah, that was great," the belayer said as she lowered me to the ground. "You got another climb on your ticket. You wanna try the kids' wall?" If she'd had any marshmallows, she probably would have passed them out to the instructors and they would have taken turns throwing them at me. Felinah's dad might have chucked a couple himself.

That day was undoubtedly the beginning and end of my illustrious rock-climbing career, but it gave me the opportunity to remember the difficulty of trying something new. You have to absorb a whole universe of unfamiliar terms (pauldron? snap? shield hook?), master the use of strange equipment (Which way are you supposed to hold that darned pole arm?), and navigate through a maze of unspoken etiquette (When do I salute?) without offending anyone too badly.

We all managed to overcome our anxieties about joining the Society at some point, but as we become more familiar with the SCA, it's easy to minimize those initial uncertainties and assume everyone is as comfortable at a tournament as we are, no matter if the goal is singing and dancing, volunteering to help with the event, or trying to survive more than two rounds of list combat.

At the next event, take a few minutes to explain what's going on to one of those people standing at the edge of the list field in trashcan armor or a polyester tunic. Give them a smile and a pat on the back. Let them know their presence is appreciated and make them feel welcome. If anyone thinks it's easy to just "jump in and get involved without feeling intimidated," I know of a great rock wall that's guaranteed to teach you a lesson.

The Christmas Crazies: Forgotten Medieval Holiday Traditions

Everywhere you look there are ecstatic smiles, twinkling lights and a relentless onslaught of cookies, cake and candy. All of this can only mean one thing: Either that low-carb diet you've clung to for the past 11 months is causing ketosis-induced hallucinations, or the holiday season is again upon us!

In some of my earlier writings we've looked at the medieval origins of modern holiday celebrations in an attempt to A) expand our understanding of ancient folklore and its affect on contemporary social customs, and B) boost sales of my holiday-themed CD. This month, however, we're going to do something just a little different—instead of examining medieval rituals that we still observe today, we're going to explore some customs and celebrations that are unique to the Middle Ages. By doing this, we'll see that, although mid-winter celebrations hundreds of years ago might seem quaint and rustic to us, they were also overindulgent, frightening and dangerous—heck, maybe they *weren't* so different from today's Christmas traditions.

So sit back, program a few Yuletide carols into "Ye Olde iPodde" and get ready for: Medieval Holiday Weirdness!

Call Me Cathy

During the Middle Ages, Christmas was celebrated over an extended period of time that began on November 25 with the Feast of St. Catherine.

Catherine was a 4th century scholar and noblewoman who gained notoriety for her devotion to the emerging Christian faith despite her life-long struggle with the nearly insurmountable handicap of being born female. Catherine was famous for her quick wit and vast intellect—she was rumored to have once triumphed in a debate with 50 pagan philosophers by issuing the rebuttal, "peto inviso procurator!" (Literally: "The Emperor wears combat boots!") In recognition of her intellectual prowess, Catherine was tortured on the wheel—one of the more horrific means of execution, even in the Roman Empire.

In order to commemorate this cheery event, the Feast of St. Catherine included all sorts of wheel-related ornaments and customs. Feasts were served on round tables, musicians sat in semi-circles and revelers danced a circular jig that involved leaping over the *Catherine's candle* while wearing long gowns made of flammable material. (Perhaps another custom for honoring St. Catherine was rubbing ointment on the guests' burns with a circular motion.)

Women who prayed for luck in courtship on St. Catherine's day could expect to be especially effective in finding a husband. Young women were supposed to ask for a man who was *opulent, libéral et agréable* (rich, generous and kind). Women over the age of 25 could pray for a man who was *soit supportable* (respectable, at least in public). And women who reached the age of 30 without a husband prayed for a man who *Un tel qu'il te plaira* (didn't smell too bad).

Although the medieval Christmas season began on St. Catharine's day, in the modern world, naturally, we realize how ludicrous it would be to start holiday festivities on November 25th. After all, what would we use to replace the "back to school" decorations if we had to wait until the end of November to put tinsel and fake snow in store windows?

Animal Instincts

As Christmas Day approached, the people of medieval Europe engaged in one of the most important aspects of the season: renewing the fertility and bounty of the natural world in the coming year. On the winter solstice the world was cold and dark, and the people felt that if they didn't give Mother Nature a kick-start, things would just continue to decline: days would get shorter, snow would get deeper, cattle would starve, TV commercial breaks would get longer and gas would become ludicrously overpriced.

So, in order to nudge the universe back in the right direction, many Christmas customs, echoing earlier pagan rites, were intended to set the stage for a prosperous new year.

To encourage the proliferation of wildlife in the forests, medieval villagers set out ornaments called *Yule Trees*, which were stalks of grain tied to tall poles. With little other food to be found amid the snow and ice, wild birds eagerly flocked to these seed-laden bundles of flora. Kissing your loved one beneath the Yule Tree could bring fortune and good luck. (And if you think about the results of necking under a flock of roosting, well-fed birds, you won't have any trouble realizing why these "kissing bushes" were soon brought indoors, suspended from the rafters and decorated with *stuffed* birds.)

Another Christmas tradition meant to stimulate bounty during the coming year was the lighting of the Bryanna's Day candle—a tradition I would like to stress, for the sake of anyone reading this chapter who happens to be the kingdom seneschal, that I'm not actually making up. Bryanna's Day was observed on the Sunday before Yule, and the traditional dinner fare on that day was: boiled cow's head (which, as God is my witness, you can still order in some of the "finer" restaurants in France). After dinner, all of the meat, skin, hair and gristle was picked off the skull, then two candles were placed in the poor cow's eye sockets. Finally, the lord of the manor went into the barn carrying this gruesome "lantern" and used the candles to singe a bit of the hair or feathers of all the cattle, horses and poultry inside. This was supposed to make the animals vigorous and fertile during the coming year—and I suppose if you had the flaming skull of one of your friends thrust at you by some murderous lunatic, you might be inspired to do anything necessary to avoid the same demise!

Similarly, the *wassailing of the trees* was an important medieval holiday custom. On Christmas Eve, all of the farmers and country folk would bundle up in their cloaks and mantles and gather 'round the oldest tree they could find, wishing it good health by singing and drinking, drinking and singing, drinking and drinking until finally they were all so overcome by cheer, merriment and frostbite that they would retire to their homes to sleep it off. Then they would wake up on Christmas morning and begin the festivities by wondering if they were *really* so drunk that they had been singing to a tree, or if it was all just a bad dream.

I'm Game If You Are

The Christmas celebration, which actually stretched from Christmas Day until Epiphany, was a time for frolicking, feasting and games. (Because, let's face it, what else are you going to do when there's a snowstorm outside and you live in a stone hut?)

One of the more popular games played on Christmas during the Middle Ages was called *bee-in-the-middle*. Bees, of all things, were actually prominent symbols of the Christmas season because the things they produced mirrored Christ's gifts to mankind: sweetness (honey) and light (beeswax for candles). To play bee-in-the-middle a person wearing a cowl resembling a bee's head sat on the floor with his feet tied up underneath him. Around the bee were seated 12 other "beekeepers" whose job it was to poke, slap, punch and generally inflict injury upon the blindfolded bee. The bee was supposed to scoot and wobble around on his knees until either A) he caught one of the beekeepers by the wrist, or B) he barfed.

Imitating animals of all kinds was a popular diversion during the Christmas season. One of the customary entertainments between courses at Yuletide feasts was the *oxhorn dance*. In order to perform this dance, a group of peasant farmers dressed up like cattle and paraded into the hall (probably not unlike today's "peasant farmers" who dress up like bulls, wolverines or ducks and parade into their local college bowl games). When the procession reached the high table, the lord of the manor put an *oxhorn cake* (a sort of stale donut) onto the horn of the lead "ox." Then, the whole group of oxen would cavort around the hall with their vision impaired by elaborate bovine masks, mooing and whooping and lacerating one another with their horns as they all tried to dislodge the oxhorn cake. Diners watching this (and trying to stay out of the way) called out "boosy!" or "istress!" depending on whether they thought the cake would roll ahead of the procession or behind it. (If they thought the procession would conclude by knocking over one of the serving tables and falling into the firepit, they probably called out, "morons!")

◆   ◆   ◆

Not all medieval Christmas customs were about singing, merrymaking and prancing around in ridiculous costumes, of course. With the longest night of year looming, people also reflected upon mortality and the spirits of their dead ancestors, who were rumored to return to their homes on the eve of the day of Yule. In order to make sure that these honored spirits would not get lost on their lonely trek, a candle was left burning in the window all night long.

An even more poignant reminder of the holiday season's contrast of joy and melancholy might be seen on Twelfth Night: At that evening's feast, an empty place setting was laid out on the table in remembrance of all the friends and relations who could join the meal in spirit only. In the midst of all the revelry, the vacant seat reminded everyone that our awareness of frailty and death are what make the fleeting moments of holiday celebrations so memorably special. *Death hangs over thee. While thou still live, while thou may, do good.*

Today, when shopping and presents threaten to eclipse friendship and community, looking back at the customs of the Middle Ages can help us to recall the meaning behind the traditions and activities we all enjoy. Whether your Christmas dinner includes roast turkey or boiled cow's head, whether you'll be playing Scrabble or bee-in-the-middle at your holiday party, the customs of the Middle Ages remind us all of how magical, marvelous and wonderfully weird the Yuletide season can be.

There Is A Hole In Your Heart

The six months of a royal reign can seem to stretch on for a long time. But of all the moments in that long six months, perhaps none is so long as the one in which you prepare to surrender the Crown—your Crown—to another. If you've been at a coronation and noticed a little pause, a slight "hitch" in the flow of the ceremony at this moment, perhaps I can give you some insight into what might be going on in the minds of the monarchs.

Before you, kneeling on the ground, are a man and a woman. Behind them is an entire kingdom that is holding its breath. The royal clock is ticking, and in just a few seconds you will remove the Crown that has made everlasting marks upon your life and your spirit—and probably even upon your head—and you will place it over the brow of this person in front of you. Then you will call that person "Your Majesty" and you will bend your knee in supplication for the first time in six months.

Those seconds stretch out for a long, long time.

What does it mean to be a king or a queen in the Society for Creative Anachronism? The SCA is just a weekend play-acting group; quite literally a costume party that began in 1966 and was too good to end. The king and queen are the hosts of the party for the duration of their reign, but they are something more than that. Party hosts are not left speechless when the party is over.

The SCA is also a non-profit corporation, and hundreds of such corporations can be found in every city in America. The king and queen are executives of a division of that corporation, but they are something more than that. Few other corporate officers have a distant, yearning look in their eyes when their term of service is complete.

Above all, the SCA is a self-contained universe, and each of its kingdoms is a bright, swirling galaxy, filled with unique planets and shining stars. For six glorious, intimidating, eternal, frantic, painful, giddy, sleepless months the king and queen are the center of that galaxy. They become the point all those planets and stars orbit gracefully around. You can relax after a party and you can retire contentedly from a term of office, but you cannot be at the center of the galaxy for six months and not be changed by the experience.

Still, there's no secret to the fact that "sitting the throne" is a lot of work. When the kingdom is tranquil, you can spend an hour or two a day sending e-mails and making phone calls. If the kingdom erupts in controversy or catastrophe, you'll find yourself using up sick-days to make enough time to conduct royal business. But the change that occurs in the wake of a reign is more than just sheer exhaustion.

That is because the job of being king and queen is more than any two people can handle. The monarchs are surrounded by trusted friends who alternately guide, advise, contemplate, contradict and simply commiserate. They are also surrounded by courtiers and guards who organize, haul, arrange, decorate, pack, maintain and repair with a level of efficiency and dedication that would put the staff at the White House to shame. And they are supported by hundreds of others who selflessly offer their talent, time, enthusiasm, material and funds, all for the sole purpose of making the king and queen the embodiment of chivalry, nobility and honor that we call *The Dream*.

All of these people deserve great rewards in return for what they give to the king and queen, but the monarchs have precious little reward to offer. They don't have chests of gold, fertile lands or lucrative offices like the royalty of old. For all of the prestige and influence that the king and queen seem to wield in the SCA, when all is said and done the only means of compensation they have at their disposal are a smile (which they hope doesn't look too weary) and a few words of thanks (which they must give quickly as they rush toward the next item on their agenda).

Yet, for all of that, the most difficult part of ruling a kingdom is not the decisions, the schedules or the meetings. The most difficult part is *letting go*. The people who have surrounded you, supported you, adorned you and kept you going when you thought you had nothing left to give—all of them will still be there the day after you step down, but the situation won't be the same. The focus and the momentum will be gone. The panic and the chaos will have evaporated. The elation and the madness will have moved on to someone else.

And what you find is that all of those things—momentum, elation, panic, and madness—created a level of trust and reliance between you and your friends that is nearly impossible to achieve any other way. It is the intimacy of soldiers who have been in battle, of explorers charting hazardous frontiers, of athletes whose teams win against-the-odds victories.

It is the kind of intimacy that people observe from outside with envious fascination, wishing they could find a way to put themselves into the crucible that forges people together in such a way. More than the presentations and the pretty outfits and the royal deference, *that* is what makes people yearn to wear the Crown.

Of course, you don't really know any of this in those long, long seconds that stand between you and the end of your reign. All you know is that in a few heartbeats the enthusiasm and dynamic energy that have inspired you to pour yourself into the kingdom will be gone.

And as you lift that Crown from your head, at last relieved of its weight, you see that a kingdom is ruled, not by two people, but by three: the king, the queen and the living entity of the Crown itself. It is the sword Excalibur, the Sangrail, the Ring of Power and the Fountain of Youth. Every monarch who has worn it has had a role in shaping its personality, but it also transcends the royal players who have stood beside it in the spotlight, and made their exits.

The Crown stirs the imagination and dominates the stage of the kingdom like an unforgettable character whose voice continues to be heard in the minds of the audience, even after the curtain has fallen.

And when you relinquish the Crown, when you pass it on to another, you are not merely giving away a symbol of state, you are ending a relationship. Some monarchs conclude that relationship like a parent sending a child away to college with hope and promise; some terminate the relationship like a rejected spouse whose eyes fill with bitter, disillusioned tears as divorce papers are signed. But all of these relationships are filled with a passion that is born of trust, pride and love.

Then, at last, the clock has ticked out. The Crown that you once called your own begins its relationship with another. As it leaves your hand, it bears away some part of your dreams, your talent, your youth and your strength. Along with the Crown goes a piece of your heart, never to be recovered. You can find satisfaction in the knowledge that a part of you will forever stand upon the stage of the kingdom, but you also know the place it was taken from will always ache—just a little bit—for its loss.

Some Knights to Remember

Recently, Felinah and I were having dinner with Baroness Kyriath. While dinner discussions between the three of us—and by "three of us" I mean "Felinah and Kyriath"—often involve subjects like "blood-sucking insects," "medieval torture instruments," or "parasitic diseases of the brain," this evening's conversation was along a slightly less gruesome topic. (Many of you may be wondering, if Kyriath insists on bringing up inappropriate, grotesque or revolting topics at the diner table, why we continue to dine with her. This is undoubtedly because you have never tasted Kyriath's chocolate mousse.)

In any case, on this particular evening, Kyriath was telling us about an article she'd read regarding literacy among knights in the Middle Ages. She explained that during medieval times, the term "literate" was used to refer specifically to someone who could read and write Latin, and who had been educated in Classical literature. "According to this," she said, "since many knights were responsible for correspondence and maintaining household accounts, probably a lot of them could actually read and write. So, really, being a fighter is no excuse for not being well-read."

Then, Felinah and Kyriath both turned and gave me a look that strongly implied that it was my, personal, fault that most SCA fighters would rather spend their Saturday afternoons getting hit in the head with a stick than reading medieval romances filled with words like "fewter" "holpen" or "overthwartly."

So, young fighters and aspiring knight-types, the time has come for me to encourage the warriors of the Known World to rise to a new level of knowledge and culture if I am to obtain what literary scholars refer to as "a second helping of chocolate mousse." What follows is a "compendium" of "medieval chivalric literature" which you should "read" in order to "educate" yourselves and dispel the perception that you are a "bone-headed rattan jockey." By doing this, you'll begin to appreciate that there's more to the Middle Ages than just armor, swords and combat. You will see that there is a rich literary tradition of stories filled to the point of obsession with descriptions of armor, swords and combat. Here, then, are some medieval works of literature which you might enjoy reading—at least during those portions of the day when it's too hot to fight.

Roland Down The River

First on any fighter's reading list should be *The Song Of Roland*, an 11th century knightly epic which is primarily distinguished by the fact that it is not, technically, a song. It is, however, an early example of the *chanson de geste*, (literally, "funny little wagon") which became quite popular in the medieval period known as "the days before sleeping pills."

The Song Of Roland describes, for approximately 4,000 lines (although at times it seems like only twice that many), the conclusion of Charlemagne's seven-year campaign against the Moors in Spain—a campaign that was so successful that that it ended with Charlemagne fleeing home to France. As Charlemagne was crossing the Pyrenees, however, he and his army were met by a large band of Moors who had come to show their appreciation for his visit by throwing a customary "arrow, rock and spear parade" to bid him farewell.

Throughout the poem, one of Charlemagne's most noble and trusted peers, Count Roland, single-handedly holds the Moors at bay with only slight assistance from Count Oliver, Count Gerer, Count Otun and about half of the French army—all of whom fight with such bravery and valor that by the end of the book dental records must be consulted to identify their bodies. The Moors are aided in their ambush by the duplicity of Ganelon, Charlemagne's evil advisor, who was probably bitter about the fact that he was, secretly, one of King Lear's daughters.

Much of the epic is concerned with the question of whether or not Roland will sound his horn. If he does, Charlemagne will hear it and return with the rest of the Frankish army. Roland does not want to play the horn, however; he wants to fight. But the other knights want Roland to play his horn. Soon, the knights begin to wonder whether or not Roland even knows *how* to play the horn. Roland assures them that he *does* know how to play the horn, and that plenty of people have seen him playing the horn, he just doesn't want to play it *right now*. The knights assure Roland that no one will think he is a sissy, artsy fighter, because he plays the horn, but Roland insists that playing the horn is not nearly as important as fighting. This debate goes on and on, causing modern scholars to wonder whether *The Song Of Roland* is, in fact, the meeting minutes from an early knights' council.

Hagen Days

The epic German poem, the *Nibelungenlied*, was written in the 13th century, and, if you began reading it at that time, you might almost be finished with it by now. As I recall from my college "Medieval and Renaissance Literature" study group, one of the most effective means of understanding the *Nibelungenlied*, from a literary standpoint is to recount the story's dynamic characters and plot in a discussion group, and every time someone says "*Nibelungenlied*," everyone in the group has to drink a shot of that renowned German beverage, tequila. I believe the resulting discussion went something like this:

"The *Nibelungenlied* is the tale of two women, Kriemhild and Brunhild. Unlike other medieval epics, the female characters of the *Nibelungenlied* have important roles, and the women of the *Nibblelunkinleed* are, in many ways, more crucial to the story than its male characters. The *Neebeelegenlan* begins with the introduction of Siegfried, who is the son of King Siegmund and Queen Siegelind. Sickfried is knighted at a huge festival in the second chapter of the *Newbielincolnlogs*, and Siegelind sends Singfried to find Lady Kriemhild so that Siegfriend can court her for his wife. Then Freegmund...wait, I mean, Frickaseed, rides with 12 warriors to find Worms and fall in love. With Kriemhild, not with the worms. Then Hagen tells the story of how Sigfreud fought the Nakedbabes and won the legendary sword Almond...Osmond...Bosley...whatever, by slaying seven giant hundreds..."

At this point, as I recall, the discussion group was so overwhelmed with the literary magnificence of the *Nibelungenlied* that many of them had to go lay down. Or throw up.

Mort And Arthur

The greatest of all chivalric literature is *Le Morte D'Arthur* which tells the story of the heroic feats of the knights of the round table. *Le Morte D'Arthur* was written in the 15th century, a romantic period of late medieval chivalric revival, by Thomas Mallory, a man who was so devoted to the causes of chivalry and romance that he spent much of his life in jail for armed robbery and rape.

Although *Le Morte D'Arthur* fills two substantial volumes, the story itself is so totally gripping and compelling that it is absolutely impossible to put it down throughout, I would estimate, the first six pages. After that, it all kinda starts to sound the same. Uther fights the Duke of Tintagel. Arthur fights the Romans. Tristram fights Breunis Saunce Pité. Lancelot fights Sir Turquin. Gawain fights Sir Marhaus. Students everywhere fight to finish this darned book before midterms...

But, in the end, the spirit of chivalry, honor and courtly love prevail, and, as Mallory so touchingly observed, "We may se all day, for a lytyll blaste of wyntres rasure, annone we shall deface and lay aparte trew love, for lytyll or nowght, that coste muche thynge."

I believe this is what he told the guards when they unlocked his cell to empty his chamber pot every morning.

◆   ◆   ◆

I hope this scholarly overview of the important works of chivalric literature will inspire everyone, fighters and non-fighters alike, to explore the many great writings of the Middle Ages. Your experience with the splendor and pageantry of the SCA will give you an insight into these books that few readers ever achieve, and, in the end, your fewter will be holpen in a more overthwartly manner than ever before. Or, if you don't believe that, you can always go back to hitting your friends with a stick.

Guillaume & Felinah—Wasn't That A Reign
or
The Last Postcard From The Throne

A quick explanation from the author: *In the course of this chapter, you'll read several passages that refer to either the king or queen "dancing naked around the fire." Kids and members of the Board of Directors, this does not mean the king and/or queen actually appeared nude in public. In this context, "naked" means "wearing belly dancing garb," which, skimpy as it may be, is a long way from being* sans *clothes. The phrase "dancing naked" is used simply to help convey the level of anxiety brought on by the prospect of middle-aged individuals appearing in fairly revealing outfits in front of two or three or a hundred of their closest friends. Rest assured, however, that the entire incident described would, at worst, have gotten a "PG" rating had it appeared on television. Now, on with the story…*

The days of autumn began to grow short, as did our time upon the thrones of Caid. Felinah and I could see light at the end of the tunnel—so close, yet still a long way off.

By this point, we'd generated over 1,200 pieces of correspondence on behalf of the kingdom—letters, phone calls and e-mails combined. We'd traveled more than 6,000 miles to conduct the business of Caid—not counting four airplane trips. During the six-month reign, we'd spent one day out of every four with Crowns on our heads.

This is nothing extraordinary. Every king and queen works just as hard as we did—if not harder. I only bring these details to your attention so you'll have some understanding of why monarchs get a little loopy toward the end of their terms, and so that history will, perhaps, be lenient in its judgment of the events that took place in the final days of our reign.

Bonfire Of The Vanities

Great Western War, held in October, was one of our last events as king and queen. Friday evening, when we were finished setting up camp, a messenger arrived to inform us that Duchess Ceinwen requested our presence. Ceinwen is the "keeper of the royal regalia," which basically means that she is the custodian of all the kingdom paraphernalia which is too obscure, old, worn-out or just plain ugly to be used on a regular basis.

When we arrived at Ceinwen's camp, she took us into her tent and showed us a box filled with what appeared to be the debris from a train derailment. She explained, however, that this collection of ripped, stained and mutilated items was the last mortal remains of a variety of royal regalia.

"Your Majesties," Ceinwen told us softly, "we normally put old regalia like this on a bonfire, quietly. It's sort of a dignified, yet discreet way to retire such items that have given great service to the kingdom. We just need your approval to dispose of this stuff. It's just a formality, really."

So, with due reverence and solemnity, we removed each item from the box just so that we'd have the honor of re-living the glory of days past one last time. We re-lived the glory of a mildewy old queen's guard tabard. We re-lived the glory of a royal banner that appeared to have been made out of a used sweatshirt and colored with a can of Krylon spray paint. We re-lived the glory of something that might have been the wreath or rosemary placed upon the brow of Caid's first prince…or, based on the size and proximity of a hole chewed in the side of the box, might have been the official Caidan royal rodent's nest. After that, we quickly re-lived the glory of packing the whole mess back into the box and getting it the heck out of there before we infested Ceinwen's tent with some type of vermin.

Ceinwen's campmates already had a bonfire burning, so we discreetly made our way to the fire and placed the first item of regalia into the flames. Since many of the people around the fire were royal peers or had served on royal courts, we knew that they would observe the event with all due dignity.

"You know, there's another royal tradition that goes along with that," said Countess Cassandra, who was sitting nearby. "The queen is supposed to dance naked around the fire as the old regalia burns. Are you going to do that?"

Fortunately Ceinwen—always a model of royal decorum—stepped in to keep things from getting out of hand. "You know, I don't really think that's appropriate. We can't have the queen skipping around in the buff. Her Majesty must maintain a certain degree of dignity. Now, the king, on the other hand…"

Then, in a move that combined the grace of a ballerina with the decibel level of an air-raid siren, Baroness Morgana—who had also been quietly observing the whole interchange—leapt to her feet, put two fingers into her mouth and whistled like a cattle rustler. "Hey, girls! Guillaume's gonna dance naked! Woo-ooo!" I can only assume that they had been planning this set-up for months, and I would have charged the whole lot of them with treason and sedition on the spot had I not suddenly found myself surrounded by a majority of the Caidan Ladies of the Rose, along with an attendant rabble of unruly baronesses and peers, all whooping, hollering, loading film into their cameras, waving dollar bills, and generally conducting themselves with a level of subtlety and restraint you don't often see outside of a Pistons play-off game.

I was beginning to fear that I had no hope of escaping from the camp with my life, if not my dignity, when I noticed a cadre of my loyal knights and vassals, attracted by the whistling and shouting, coming to my rescue. Ciaran, Gavin, Padraic and Thorvald gathered around the growing crowd of Ladies of the Rose, and, as they learned the tragic fate that was about to befall their king, I could see them wiping away tears of sorrow as they doubled over and knelt upon the ground in anguish.

Hey, wait a minute, I thought. *Those guys are laughing!*

"All right you #@*&$," I yelled over the growing din, "Last time I checked, you're all in fealty to me, and I'm not dancing by myself—get over here!" Which, of course, brought another round of cheering from the out-of-control ladies—including my own dear queen, who *claimed* that she was not doing anything to encourage this behavior, but who somehow mysteriously wound up in a front-row seat with a handful of dollar bills and a can of pressurized whipped cream.

So, my vassals, having been relieved of strategic portions of their clothing, reluctantly joined me dancing and cavorting around the fire as the assembled Ladies of the Rose began screaming and clapping and lighting cigars and flinging various items of undergarments as they piled more and more regalia on the fire. I was pretty sure things couldn't get any worse when I suddenly realized that several of these frenzied Ladies of the Rose were busily engaged in putting chocolate-filled gold coins down my pants.

WARNING TO FUTURE MONARCHS: Do NOT let frenzied Ladies of the Rose put chocolate-filled gold coins down your pants. This is not an appropriate, nor particularly hygienic way of treating the Sovereign Monarch of the Realm, a fact which I discovered later that evening as I was leaning over a bucket of water inside my tent while Felinah attempted to shave approximately three pounds of congealed Godiva chocolate out of the hair on the back of my knees...

Fortunately, Earl Gar was passing by at the time and, spying our predicament, took action to save us regardless of the very real danger of being molested by a variety of ex-Queens of Caid whose judgment had been impaired by estrogen, rum and chocolate. As we were dancing around the fire, trying to shake candy coins out of our respective shorts, Gar pranced through a gap in the crowd and became the Emergency Bail-Out Sugar Plum Fairy, dancing the knights one-by-one away from the fire, out of camp and into a nearby FBI safe house where federal agents were waiting to help them establish new identities as members of a tribe of cliff-dwelling natives in Belize.

Needless to say, I was the last one left dancing, and I was pretty sure that the rest of the guys would pay Gar top-dollar to leave me out there to be mauled by the ladies. However, just when things were starting to look really grim, Gar returned one last time, leaping and pirouetting like Rudolph Nureyev, and whisked me away to safety. As we slipped into the surrounding darkness, I realized that the flickering light had not been caused by the bonfire, but by approximately 70,000 camera flashes being operated by a crowd of spectators who had gathered in a mob stretching from the road beside the camp to approximately the border of An Tir.

Thank goodness, I thought to myself, we were able to fulfill our Royal mission in the dignified, yet discreet manner which was called for in this situation.

Majesty Of Caid, White Courtesy Phone

My last opportunity to represent Caid on the "inter-kingdom SCA scene" was at the Estrella treaty negotiations, which occur in Atenveldt on the last weekend in October. By this time, the reserves of strength, preparation and good judgment were running low—not just in myself, but in all of the advisors and attendants around me as well.

Since Felinah had to attend a tournament in Caid, she couldn't go to the negotiations, and, thus, my arrangements were not quite as organized as they might have been. Duke Arthur of Atenveldt had graciously offered to play host to the "Caidan contingent," so we all hoped that this would be an easy, stress-free trip. Sure, we were all tired, distracted and irritable. Sure, we may have made some questionable judgment calls. Sure, our travel plans might have been somewhat creative and unstructured, but I figured we were all going to the same place for the same reason, and that things would work out—so sue me.

At this time, I would like to clear up some vicious rumors that sprang up following the negotiations:

First, let me say that my traveling companion, Baron Thorvald, and I did *not* get on a plane, fly into the Phoenix Sky Harbor international airport, rent a car and drive for more than 25 miles with "no idea whatsoever" where Duke Arthur lived, how we were going to get there, or even how to get in contact with His Grace.

Second, we did *not* drive to the most popular nightspot we could locate in downtown Phoenix with the sole intention of finding a Mexican restaurant serving 99-cent "King Kong margaritas" during happy hour—which apparently lasts until 3 a.m. in Arizona.

Third, the effects of said margaritas did *not* cause Thorvald and I to forget that we were supposed to meet Prince Ivan's incoming flight later that evening, and we certainly did *not* leave the Royal Heir of Caid "stranded" in the airport where His Highness spent approximately three and a half hours entertaining himself by begging strangers for cigars and coffee while Thorvald and I attended a screening of the movie *Blair Witch 2*.

And finally, the Kingdom Seneschal and the Earl Marshal did *not* have the King of Caid paged over the airport public-address system so that they could find out where we were, what we were doing, and if there was any prayer we were going to arrive at Duke Arthur's house at some point before dawn.

I hope this dispels any misconceptions. I know I speak for the entire Caidan contingent when I say that we were proud to represent our kingdom at this important event. I'm not sure how these rumors got started, but I hope that all of my readers will be somewhat skeptical of any stories being told by a former chamberlain and a sanctimonious ex-queen claiming that their preparations for the tournament the following day were interrupted by the task of conducting an *X Files*-style interstate manhunt for a missing king and an errant Calafian baron.

The End Of Daze

One of the first proclamations I made after winning Crown Tournament was that we would absolutely, positively, *no way* have one of those weepy, emotional stepping down ceremonies where the king and queen spend several hours crying and hugging and drooling all over their courtiers, guards, advisors, assistants, consultants, taste-testers, lion tamers, U-boat pilots and other random people who somehow to get appointed to the royal court.

This was very ironic. It was an indication that, both at the beginning and the end of our reign, I had no idea what I was doing.

Our stepping down was very nice—or so I'm led to believe. I don't remember a whole lot of it. I was too busy crying, hugging and drooling on people. I do know that reaching the end of our reign was the most terrible and wonderful thing I could imagine. I could not have survived one more week of it. I also wanted it to go on forever.

To all those fighters out there who think (like I did) they'll never be good enough, strong enough or talented enough to win the Crown—don't give up. If a goofy, clumsy, latté-drinking, column-writing sissy knight can make it to the throne, so can you. It takes some work, but trust me, the view is worth the climb.

To all those lords and ladies out there who wonder (like I did) whether you're worthy to wear the mantle of state—you are. Courtesy, grace and generosity are the marks of true royalty, and these virtues reside within everyone who yearns for the romance and ideals of days of yore. Your smile can conquer a kingdom more effectively than any sword or army.

And to all those people out there who roll their eyes (like I used to) at the thought of sitting through *another* royal stepping down—be patient. Your king and queen have been through a lot. They have seen the best and worst the SCA has to offer. For the past 180 days they have surfed the colossal tsunami wave of all time, and their lives have been a constant mix of terror and euphoria. Through it all, they've been surrounded, supported and given strength to endure beyond endurance by all those people they're up there hugging, crying and drooling on today. And they're wondering if they're going to have any friends left tomorrow, when the tsunami has slipped out from under them. Your presence at this transition is more meaningful than you know. Be patient.

For six months, the king and queen, their captain, their chamberlain and all of their attendants are thrown together under impossible conditions to do an impossible task. Each day is a battle against the forces of exhaustion, self-importance, despair, ego, chaos, frustration, complacency, and delusion. But we have, we do, and we will continue to triumph in those battles to prove that any man can become a king, that within every woman there is a queen, and that inside every heart lives The Dream.

May it be so from now until the end of time.

Long live the King and Queen.

Finale

All I own for another moment of time…

Those are the words Queen Elizabeth I muttered with her last breath, or so the rumor goes. Time isn't kind to either kings or authors, and I'm afraid the time has come once more to say farewell, even though there are still many wonderful stories to be told. But although time may not be the author's ally, it is a friend to the inhabitants of the Current Middle Ages—because as long as there is time, there will be places to go, stories to tell and friends to share them with.

Which is good, because as you know if you paid close attention to the finale of my previous book, I didn't get to all the stories I promised to tell in book number two. That's the curse of the storyteller. (Of course, it would also be the motto of a good troubadour: "Don't use up all your material in one sitting.") So, hang in there; in my third book, I'll tell you the stories of the mud-soaked baroness and the waterproof count, why Master William Blackfox kicked me out of his pavilion, the perfectly good king who got thrown away, and the day the barony burned down.

Until then, celebrate the spirit of chivalry, and cherish the time that is yours…

About the Author

Scott Farrell...

is an author, actor and speaker living in Southern California. His articles have appeared in many magazines and websites, including *Renaissance Magazine, Chivalry Sports, The Funny Times, Advance, Police Magazine, The Informant* and *Troynovant.com*. In 2003 he appeared as one of the principle players in the La Jolla Stage Company's production of *The Complete Works of William Shakespeare (abridged)*. He gives presentations on *Leadership Principles of the Code of Chivalry* to businesses, civic groups and sports teams all across the country as part of the Chivalry Today educational program. His syndicated column, *Medieval Merriment with Sir Guillaume*, appears monthly in several SCA kingdom newsletters.

Duke Guillaume de la Belgique...

is an early 14th century French nobleman who is a blatant practitioner of Bogomilism (look it up). His primary vocation is trying to drag the rest of his household out of the Dark Ages and into a civilized culture where everyone walks upright and wears *cotehardies*. He is a member of the Order of Chivalry, the Order of the Pelican, former landed Baron of Calafia and a duke. He resides in Calafia with his wife, Duchess Felinah Tifarah Arnvella Memo Hazara Khan-ad-Din.

www.SirGuillaume.com

Visit the official website of Sir Guillaume to find:
- Hilarious stories about medieval history and SCA life (many never-before published);
- Poems, papers and essays by a variety of guest authors and friends;
- The on-line store where you can purchase more books, CDs and other worthless junk.

And watch for Guillaume's next book, *War Correspondent of the Current Middle Ages*, coming soon…

www.ChivalryToday.com

A unique, insightful exploration of the Code of Chivalry in the modern world, including:
- Applications of the Seven Knightly Virtues in business, sports and politics;
- Examinations of chivalry through media and popular culture;
- Stories of real-life heroes and role models.

Join the ongoing quest for courtesy, honor and chivalry in the 21st century, with no membership fees or premium content charges. *Chivalry Today is an educational program that operates on generous donations from the public.*

0-595-34686-3

Printed in the United States
108718LV00004B/80/A